AF412464

OAK KNOLL SERIES
on
THE HISTORY OF THE BOOK

The Art of Book-Binding,
Its Rise and Progress;
Including a Descriptive
Account of the New York
Book-Bindery
and
The Great New-York
Book-Bindery

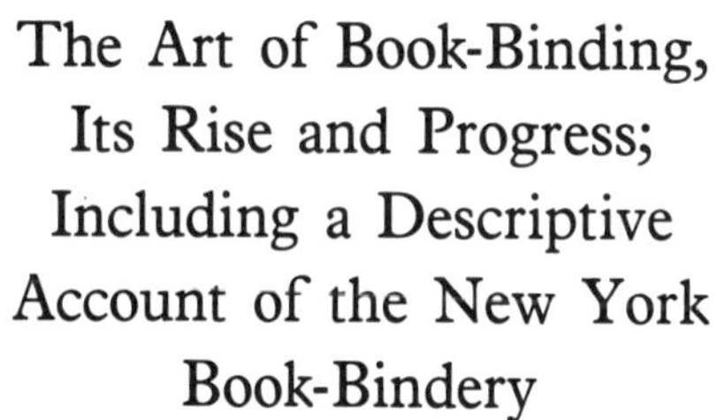

The Art of Book-Binding,
Its Rise and Progress;
Including a Descriptive
Account of the New York
Book-Bindery

BY EDWARD WALKER

and
The Great New-York
Book-Bindery

Edited with an Introduction by
PAUL S. KODA

OAK KNOLL BOOKS
NEW CASTLE
1984

Note on facsimile: This photo-reprint has been made from a copy in the Library of the University of North Carolina at Chapel Hill with permission.

Library of Congress Cataloging in Publication Data

Walker, Edward, 1804–1879.

The art of book-binding. Its Rise and Progress; Including a Description and Account of the New York Book-Bindery and The Great New-York Book-Bindery.

(The Oak Knoll series on the history of the book.) Edited with introduction and index by Paul S. Koda. Reprint (1st work). Originally published: New York : E. Walker, 1850.

Reprint (2nd work). Originally published: New York: J. Walker, 188-?

1. Bookbinding. 2. Bookbinding—New York (N.Y.)—History. I. Koda, Paul S. (Paul Stephen), 1942–   . II. Great New-York Book-Bindery. 1984. III. Title. IV. Series.

Z269.W213 1984   686.3   84-5242

ISBN 938768-07-7

The following institutions have generously given permission to include materials from their collections: Walker's trade card (fig. 2) and advertisement for the New York Book-Bindery (fig. 3), published with permission of the General Research Division, The New York Public Library, Astor, Lenox and Tilden Foundations; *The Great New-York Book-Bindery*, published with permission of Columbia University Library. This book has been designed by Henry Morris of the Bird & Bull Press.

Printed on acid-free, 200-year-life paper in the United States of America.

Oak Knoll Books, 414 Delaware Street, New Castle, Delaware 19720

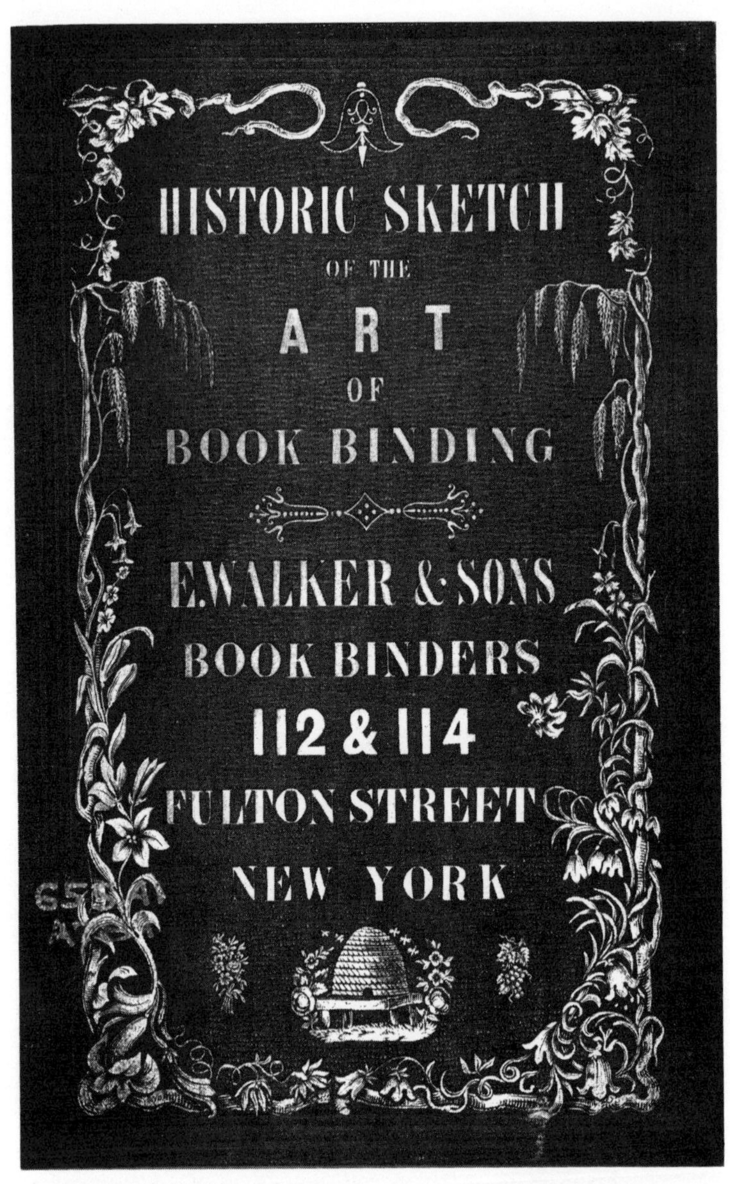

Figure 1. Upper Cover of *The Art of Book-Binding*

Introduction

The craft and art of binding books underwent major changes in England and in the United States during the first half of the nineteenth century. Large numbers of books were no longer bound by hand individually to order as they had been in preceding centuries; instead they were cased in uniform lots. In the 1820s traditional leather covers began to give way to cloth covers, which were plain and drab in the 1820s and 1830s, but often highly decorated by the middle of the century. As the reading public grew larger and more diversified, more and more covering materials and styles were invented and used, and binding factories began to displace the small shop as the size of publishers' editions increased to meet the heavy demand for information and entertainment.

All these changes were part of and caused by the burgeoning Industrial Revolution in England. Because of close cultural and commercial ties with England, the United States often adopted English manufacturing techniques, and bookbinding methods were no exception. One notable difference, however, was in the publication of information about binding books. Though several bookbinding manuals and handbooks had been published in England before 1850, no separately published American work on bookbinding seems to have appeared in the United States before 1850. In that year Edward Walker published under his own name the book reprinted here: *The Art of Book-Binding, Its Rise and Progress; Including a Descriptive Account of the New York Book-Bindery* (New York: E. Walker & Sons, 1850).

As it turns out, even *The Art of Book-Binding* has English origins; Walker borrowed much of its contents from early nineteenth-century English bookbinding manuals. Walker also had personal ties to England: he was born in London in 1804 and may have started a binding business there in the 1820s (a bookbinder named Edward Walker had a shop at 5 Silver Street, Wood Street [*sic*] in 1828 [21, p. 144]). He immigrated to the United States in 1832 or 1833 and soon after his arrival began binding books in New York City. But he maintained his English ties throughout his life, often by means of extended return visits. In 1851, for example, he and his wife, Sophia, were very much the tourists when they spent two summer months in London visiting the "enchanted" Great Exhibition "almost daily" [32, p. 6]. This visit was a combination of business and pleasure (Walker's contribution to the Great Exhibition is discussed below), but other trips nurtured family and personal relationships that Walker obviously wanted to keep up. He made at least one more lengthy trip to England (five months in 1867), and a lifelong English friend, invited to New York as a companion for Walker's daughter in 1871, became his second wife, Emily, in 1872 [33]. His last journey to England was in 1874 [34]; he died in Yonkers, 11 January 1879 [28].

The young Walker's first few years in New York were ones of rapid change, to judge from his different business addresses. In 1835 he was at 121 Chapel Street; in 1836 at 200 Broadway; in 1837 at 75 Barclay; and in 1838 at 112 Fulton [15].[1] In 1842 or 1843 Walker complied with "the wishes of numerous friends and patrons" by opening "an auxiliary to his well known Cheap and Substantial Bookbinding Establishment" that was at 112 Fulton Street; the new store was at 114 Fulton Street and was called "Edward Walker's Cheap Bookbinding, Bookselling, and Stationary Store" [27]. It served as an attractive retail outlet for the bindery, for as Walker says, "Ladies will now find it easy to call and give their orders for the neat and fancy binding of their Music, Albums, Scrap Books, etc." [27].

The 112-114 Fulton Street address was to remain the location of the bindery until 1871 when it moved to 55 Dey Street and then to 14 Dey in 1877, two years before his death. The imprint on the title page of *The Art of Book-Binding* shows that Walker's sons, James Edward and Joseph Edward, had officially joined the firm by 1850. The father's remark that his "two sons, who have been trained under his special care, aided by talented instructors, are now in partnership" indicates the partnership was of recent formation [p. 47].

The partnership probably gave Walker the time he needed to expand his interest in publishing books, an interest that began to gain momentum in the second half of the 1840s. Walker seems to have published only two or three dozen titles; and even though some of his advertising emphasizes publishing more than binding (see fig. 2), the bindery was his main commercial and financial enterprise. An idea of the size of the New York Book-Bindery in the early 1850s can be gained from a newspaper description of a fire that destroyed it in 1852: "The fire originated in the bindery of E. Walker, in the fourth stories of the buildings of Nos. 112 and 114 Fulton-street. . . . Mr. Walker also occupied the second story of No. 114, and of all his vast stock, we cannot find that one article

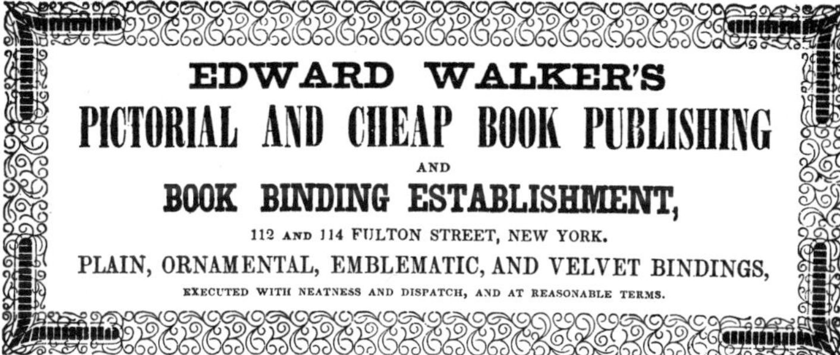

Figure 2. Walker's "Trade Card" (1847)

has been saved. The bindery was one of the most extensive in the city, and the loss to Mr. W. must be about $35,000, on which there was but only $5,000 insurance" [19]. Walker made a rapid recovery from the fire, and the bindery continued to support him, his two sons, and their families. In contrast to his publishing, the bindery was the business that remained longest at particular locations and the one that appears consistently from year to year in the New York City directories; his name as a publisher appears and disappears almost whimsically. (See the Appendix for more information about Walker's publishing.)

In spite of the disastrous fire, Walker's enterprises flourished through the 1850s, then began to fluctuate in the mid-1860s, as he began to approach later life. He is listed as a binder in the 1865 city directory, but in 1866 only his home address is recorded [25]. This may have been a trial year of retirement or partial retirement, for in 1867 he is once more listed as a binder. In 1869 the title of president is added to that of binder; this appellation is not recorded again, but he most likely continued to hold the position. The 1874 directory is the last to list an occupation and a business address for him. Only his home address is reported in 1875, the year that may have marked the beginning of his full retirement. He moved his residence to Yonkers that October [33]. By the 1870s Walker was no longer publishing many books, and his remaining stock was distributed by C. H. Jones [1]. After his retirement, his two sons assumed the responsibility of running the bindery. They inherited it after his death in 1879, and at least one Walker seems to have operated the bindery until 1892, when it went out of business [25].

What kind of man was Walker? Although little information about him seems to have survived, obituaries and his prefaces to the works he published provide the outlines of his public personality. He matches our image of the typical enterprising nineteenth-century American. He "built up a prosperous book-binding and publishing business . . . from which he was able to retire with a competency . . . leaving his two sons to carry it on" [31], and took an active part in the manufacturing and business affairs of the city, holding "many prominent positions in the American Institute and other associations" and serving as trustee of the Bowery Savings Bank [30]. He was also a "man of liberal views and of unbounded charity" with great affection for his "adopted country" [30]. He held a deep Christian faith, as shown through a long association with the Odd Fellows, and was devoted to his family [32].

But all was not sweetness and light. After Walker died, his elder son, Joseph, contested his father's will. Walker had left the Fulton Street building and land, "all my certain lot of land with the building thereon, and the appurtenances thereunto belonging, known as number one hundred and fourteen Fulton Street," in trust to his widow and daughters, mainly, it seems, to insure an income for them after his death [29]. Even though the sons inherited the remainder of the substantial estate, including Walker's one-third share in the bindery (which had been moved to Dey Street some years previously), they felt they should claim the Fulton Street property and its rentals as well. The testimony of Walker's widow at the hearing to settle the dispute reveals more of the family situation:

In '71 I was living in N.Y. at Mr. Walker's residence. Members of family at that time were an Aunt Sister [*sic*] & one single daughter. Moved to Yonkers in Oct. '75. Have liv.d there since. Since year '75 the relations between father and eldest son were friendly to time of his death—the estrangement between father and second son existed before I became a member of [the] family. There was a great disappointment on part of dec.d with regard to his son James. He was disappointed that he had been an unkind son to him.[2] [33]

On examining Walker's published writings, it is not easy to

13

tell what is truly Walker and what is simply the high-flown rhetoric of the Victorian style of writing. The personal observations he makes show a public personality that is optimistic, hearty, vigorously enthusiastic, and business-minded. Part of his business ability was a talent for seizing or developing occasions to promote his binding and publishing activities. This is clearly evident in the opening sentence of his Preface to *The Art of Book-Binding*: "This little manual, descriptive of the origin and progress of book-binding, has been prepared by the publisher, expressly for the use of his numerous patrons, in the belief that it will be found to comprise much curious and interesting matter relative to the bibliopegistic art, which will prove acceptable to all true lovers of books" [p. vii]. Ostensibly, Walker's purpose for writing the book was to provide information about bookbinding. But by addressing the work directly to his "patrons"—that is, customers of the firm— Walker indicates that the "interesting matter relative to the bibliopegistic art" has to do specifically with his New York Book-Bindery. This is supported by the publishing history of the book. It was not copyrighted, and Walker never seems to have offered it for sale in any of the many advertisements for his books that were printed in his publications. It is likely, then, that he used *The Art of Book-Binding* as a promotional gift.[3] But it was a gift designed to educate his customers about the history and techniques of bookbinding as well as a means of introducing them to the workings and wares of his New York Book-Bindery.

Walker's commercial aims go far towards explaining the composition of the book. Like many other nineteenth-century authors, Walker did not hesitate to borrow from earlier published works. And what he does and does not borrow reveals his own views on bookbinding. To better understand Walker's views it helps to know that he divided the book into three major sections: selections on the early history of books; a detailed description of how books are bound; and a description of his bindery and the services it offered.

The first section of *The Art of Book-Binding* (pages 13-24) is not a history of early books but rather a compilation of anecdotes and miscellaneous facts about the production and publication of books in earlier centuries. Walker himself calls this first section a collection of a "few brief notices of the early scribes, illuminators, and publishers," which he considers "introductory to the following sketch of the book-binding art" [p. 13]. None of this historical information was new to Walker's readers; it was available in books and articles that had already been published. And very little of it is useful to readers today, for much of it has been superseded by subsequent research.

Even so, it is interesting to see what Walker does with the material. He is less interested in providing a thorough history of early books than he is in stressing the great value and importance attached to books in times past. Books were so highly regarded that deliberate efforts were made to make them beautiful:

So precious were manuscripts in those days, that an Anglo-Saxon bishop, named Wilfred, had the books of the four evangelists copied out in letters of gold upon purple parchment; and such value did he set upon the work when it was completed, that he kept it in a case of gold adorned with precious stones. [p. 20]

As Walker points out, and as one would expect from him, the regard for the text in those early days was so high that the means of protecting it, whether in a secure case or in a binding, required the same attention that was given to the text itself: "Good books, it has been well observed, deserve good binding" [p. viii]. He is quick to observe that books in the middle of the nineteenth century are no longer as scarce and expensive as they were in medieval times: "books were then

. . . rare and costly luxuries—the prerogative of the privileged few; now they have become the common property of mankind" [p. 14]. Yet the modern accessibility of books does not diminish the importance of the book *qua* book; Walker emphasizes that books still deserve the same lavish protection they received formerly. Luckily, the manufacturing inventiveness of the nineteenth century makes it possible to have beautiful books at a very low price:

Thanks to the invention of "the divine art" [i.e., printing] and the agency of steam, we now may multiply books to an almost unlimited extent, and at an incredibly trifling expense. The rich and elaborate illuminations of the laborious monks and scribes of olden times we also re-produce in all their gorgeousness and splendor, at almost a fraction of their original cost. The same remark applies with equal force to the external decorations in binding of books; the most exquisite skill having been evinced in the emblematic devices lavished upon them. [pp. 23–24]

We learn later that his New York Book-Bindery can provide this service very well.

Once Walker has persuaded his readers that attractive covers are a requisite for binding books, he turns to the way books are bound. If there has been any doubt about whether there were similarities between American and English binding practices in the mid-nineteenth century, this second section of *The Art of Book-Binding* (pages 24–41) should dispel them. Walker uses descriptions, sometimes word-for-word, from English binding manuals published earlier in the century, to describe the manufacturing practices in his own bindery.[4]

The second section of *The Art of Book-Binding* is illustrated with five wood engravings. As with the text, Walker borrowed heavily; at least four of the five had been published as early as 1842, in Charles Knight's *Penny Magazine* [13].[5]

Knight's Illustrations	*Walker's Corresponding Illustrations*
"Sewing-Press," p. 379	Sewing Press and Sewer, p. 32
"Rounding the Back of a Book," p. 380	Rounding the Back and Finisher, p. 34
"Board-cutting Machine," p. 381	Board-cutting Machine, p. 35
" 'Extra-Finisher' at work," p. 384	Extra-finisher at Work, p. 38

Walker also borrowed another illustration from Knight: the frontispiece to *The Art of Book-Binding.* Knight's engraving is entitled "Roan-binding Shop.—Messrs. Westleys and Clark's Factory" [13, p. 377], but Walker did not hesitate to copy it exactly in all its minute detail and relabel it "The New York Book-Bindery."

Two of Knight's illustrations do not appear in Walker's book. One shows a "Cloth-embossing Machine" [13, p. 383], which Walker does not mention. His bindery probably did not have a machine for embossing cloth. This is understandable because the New York Book-Bindery specialized in covering materials such as leather or velvet (see fig. 3), which were not embossed. Walker's bindery also specialized in pictorial decorations that were stamped or blocked individually on book covers, either in gold or in blind. This latter method of decorating a cover was done on another kind of press. Knight shows such a press in the second illustration that does not appear in Walker's book. Knight calls it an "Embossing-Press" [13, p. 384]. It is a tall machine with an upper horizontal flywheel that is spun by two men in order to move a platen up and down; Knight tells the reader that Westleys and Clark has "three embossing-presses . . . situated in the basement," which "are of immense power," one exerting "a pressure of no less than *eighty tons*" [13, p. 383, Knight's emphasis]. Here Walker has substituted an illustration showing a machine that has the same purpose, which he calls an "embossing machine" [p. 36].[6] Unlike the one shown by Knight, Walker's machine has two vertical wheels that activate a toggle joint that forces a platen up against a die. Like Knight, Walker also wants to impress the reader with the force of the machine: "It is of immense pressure, sometimes amounting to fifty tons. Two of these beautiful machines, costing $1000 each, constructed by Adams [Isaac Adams, 1802–1883] of Boston, are constantly in use in the above establishment. They are both worked and heated by steam, and are capable of producing about eighteen impressions each an hour" [p. 36].[7]

Even though the second section of *The Art of Book-Binding* contains most of the volume's illustrations, there are three others worth mentioning because they are signed by important American artists of the day. The title-page vignette of the bindery and the montage of antique books and scrolls at the head of the text on page 13 are signed by the noted American wood engraver and art dealer Samuel Putnam Avery (1822–1904). Whether it was Putnam himself or his assistant, Isaac Pesoa, who executed the engravings is unclear, but the location of Avery's firm at 129 Fulton Street during this period suggests a close relationship between Walker and Avery [6, 1850]. The second artist whose name appears on a wood engraving (the floral wreath on the page after the title leaf) is Benson John Lossing (1813–1891). Like Avery, Lossing had his working establishment near Walker's bindery, at 71 Nassau Street [6, 1850]. Although Lossing's name does not mean as much today as Avery's does, he was well known in the nineteenth century as an author, editor, and wood engraver. He established his reputation in the early 1850s with the publication of his *Pictorial Field-book of the Revolution* (New York: Harper, 1850–1852), which began appearing the same year as Walker's *Art of Book-Binding*.[8]

18

NEW YORK BOOK BINDERY,

114 Fulton street, New York.

☞ This old establishment is chiefly devoted to the finer and more costly styles of Book-binding in—**TURKEY MOROC-CO, RUSSIA, ENGLISH, FRENCH,** and **AMERICAN CALF,** and especially those unique and economical half Calf and Morocco styles. In all cases the very best of *Stock* and *Workmanship*, with *strength* and *beauty* combined, may bo relied upon.

Large Illustrated Works, Books of Engravings, Scrap-Books,

ALBUMS, PORTFOLIOS, AND MUSIC,

BOUND WITH GREAT CARE AND STRENGTH, IN PLAIN AND ELEGANT STYLES.

E. W. returns his thanks to his friends and the public for the favors they have so liberally bestowed on him for upwards of twelve years, and he takes this opportunity to inform them that he has very considerably enlarged and improved his Establishment, which he believes to be as extensive, and to possess as great facilities as any Book-bindery in the United States.

His two Sons, who have been reared under his special care and Talented Instructors, in the Art of Book-Binding, are now in partnership with him, and they confidently hope, by their united attention and experience, to give good satisfaction to their patrons; who may rest assured no expense will be spared in the adoption of every improvement, the employment of the highest grade of Workmen, and the most careful selection of Stock, and in all instances, the most reasonable Scale of Prices will be adopted.

*** It is highly advantageous to GENTLEMEN HAVING LIBRARIES, and for LITERARY INSTITUTIONS, to

APPLY DIRECT TO THIS ESTABLISHMENT.

They will effect a saving of TWENTY PER CENT., and sometimes more.

N. B —Gentlemen residing at a distance, experiencing difficulty in getting their Binding done, will find it to their advantage to pack and direct them as above, statings tyle and price; they may rely upon their being well bound, at the lowest prices, and carefully packed and returned without delay. In all such cases the owner to be charged with freight, and an order for payment for the binding, on a bank or firm in New York, is required. The owners of books thus sent, are requested to state expressly the route by which they wish them to be returned.

Music bound on an improved principle, with Patent Spring Backs, in neat and elegant bindings.

A PROOF OF THE POPULARITY OF THIS ESTABLISHMENT.

☞ 5 0 0 0   C O P I E S ☜

of Messrs. Harpers' PICTORIAL BIBLE and SHAKSPEARE have been bound in Splendid Pictorial patterns at this Bindery.

E. W. and Sons particularly invite the attention of Librarians, and gentlemen having Libraries, to their extensive Binding Establishment, possessing every facility for the best of workmanship, expedition, and low prices. Reviews and Magazines bound to pattern.

N. B. — The Subscribers beg to assure their friends and the public, that their orders will receive particular attention, and that the style and workmanship shall equal any binding done either in England, France, or America.

E. WALKER & SONS,
114 FULTON STREET, NEW YORK.

Figure 3. Advertisement in the *Young People's Mirror* (1848)

By employing outstanding book illustrators Walker helped to insure the sale of his books. He had the added advantage of being able to provide at cost many styles of binding that would make a single title attractive to various segments of the buying public. Walker used this wide choice of styles to market his books, but he was also proud of his bindery's work for less pragmatic reasons and thought it contributed to binding innovation. This can be seen in the description of the Bible he placed in competition at the Great Exhibition held in London in 1851:

This Bible, in two volumes, from the foundation of the binding, has been carefully executed, especially as regards to flexible backs. One hundred and twelve engravings are in the books, which are all guarded on satin, preventing the plate paper from cracking, and at the same time making an easy hinge for the engravings to open upon. Every signature or section is sewed with strong silk and bound round the bands from end to end, making it a very elaborate piece of sewing. The volumes are also forwarded in the most flexible style, in reference to the backs, so that if the backs are turned inside out they will return without the slightest injury. The style is antique, one volume bearing the model of the tower of Magdalen College, Oxford. There is one especial feature in this Bible deserving notice: the family record, which is altogether on a new plan, being inserted in the lids, each lid containing two original designs. [14, p. 1441]

There were seven entries in the American bookbinding category at the Great Exhibition; even though Walker's binding only earned an Honourable Mention (described as "furnished articles of manufacture which, without reaching a high degree of excellence, are interesting as examples of the processes or present condition of the trades which they illustrate"), he was still the only entrant who took the trouble to describe the style and structure of his binding [22, p. v].

The kinds of bindings and services available from the New York Book-Bindery are described in the third part of *The Art of Book-Binding* (pages 44–49, the remainder of the text). The range of materials and styles of ornamentation offered by the firm was wide: "Every variety of plain and ornamental binding is here executed in muslin, sheep, roan, English, French, and American calf, russia, vellum, morocco, velvet, and the inlaid or illuminated styles, as well as those unique and economic styles in half calf and morocco" [p. 46]. The manufacturing process was flexible enough to accommodate the "single volume" [p. 45] or an "entire library" [p. 44] and yet sufficiently mechanized to execute large edition binding for publishers with ease: "By an admirable distribution of labor in this establishment, large editions of any work, consisting of even 10,000 volumes, can be produced in muslin or sheep binding, in an incredibly short space of time, and in the best possible manner" [p. 45]. The management was also willing to serve institutional collections: "Librarians connected with colleges and other public institutions, will find it a matter of great economy to apply *direct* to this establishment, as they will thereby effect a saving of twenty per cent., and sometimes more—a deduction of price being made upon large orders so consigned" [p. 46, Walker's emphasis].

Between the second and third parts of *The Art of Book-Binding* (pages 41–44), Walker talks about binding styles. Though the New York Book-Bindery willingly offered a variety of services to many kinds of customers, its primary interest was in fancy bindings: "this establishment . . . is chiefly devoted to the more elegant and costly styles of book-binding, in its several varieties of velvet, turkey, morocco, russia, calf, and sheep binding, etc." [pp. 41–42].[9] The origin of the decorations produced by Walker's bindery was the "gorgeous designs of the Gothic ages" [p. 43]—hence his preliminary remarks on medieval bindings. Walker readily acknowledged the pervasive influence of medieval decorative styles during the mid-Victorian period and was keenly aware of the cultural developments that fashioned prevailing attitudes of accepted design. He understood, for example, the importance that Owen Jones (1809–1874), an advocate of medieval design and the superintendent of the Great Exhibition of 1851, had in setting standards of decoration: "great credit is due to the laborious research and artistic skill of Mr. Owen Jones, whose numerous and superb specimens of the illuminations of the medieval epoch evince such surpassing beauty in their dazzling contrast of coloring, and splendor of the art of printing in gold and silver" [p. 44].

In spite of his appreciation of Jones and like-minded ornamental designers, Walker was not entirely convinced of the appropriateness of medieval binding styles for nineteenth-century bindings. Some medieval styles, he thought, were "grotesquely . . . adorned" [p. 42], and he wondered whether the new manufacturing inventions and technology of the nineteenth century were not capable of developing their own designs, rather than depending so heavily on the past: "How far this preference for the antique is likely to become permanently popular it is difficult to decide. It is, we think, not improbable that it will in a short time give place to a standard of taste more in unison with the modern arts of design" [pp. 43–44].[10] Unfortunately, Walker never explains what he means by "modern arts of design." It is not obvious from his bindings what these might be, for his bindings are generally quite typical of the mid-nineteenth century. One difference, however, may be his tendency to use more "elaborate pictorial and emblematic" [p. 45] features than his contemporaries. Certainly the strong pictorial and emblematic features of his bindings are particularly Victorian; they reflect the narrative realism that was characteristic of art and literature in the middle of the nineteenth century. A good example of Walker's use of emblems is the beehive on the upper cover of *The Art of Book-Binding* (fig. 1). It is a centuries-old emblem of the unified Christian community, undoubtedly of interest to Walker

Figure 4a. Lossing's *Seventeen Hundred and Seventy-Six* (1847)

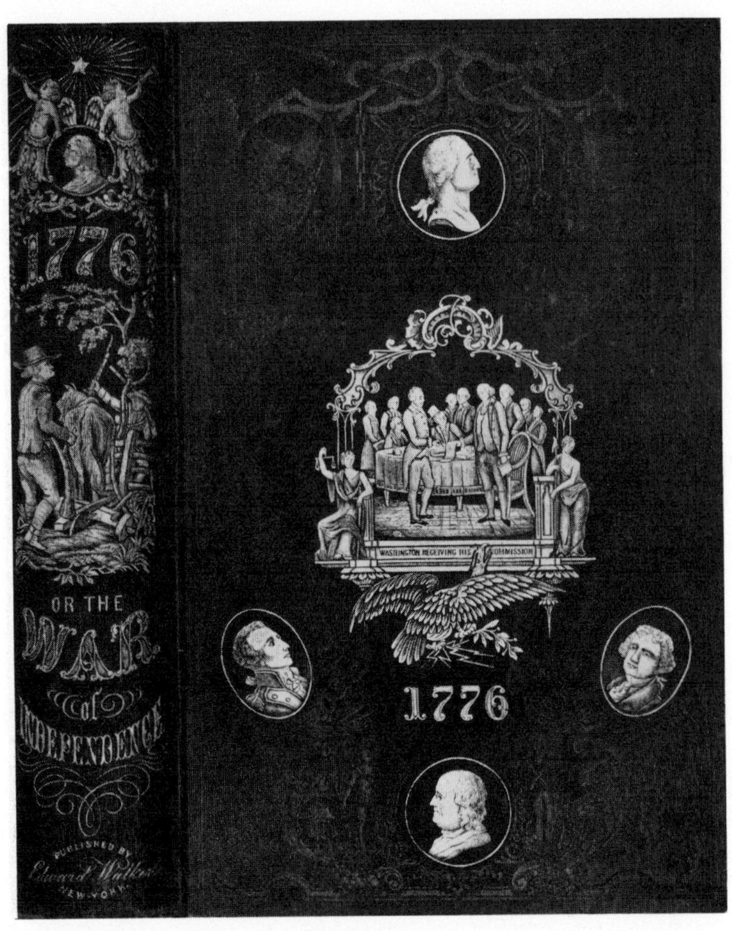

Figure 4b. Lossing's *Seventeen Hundred and Seventy-Six* (1847)

because of his membership in the Odd Fellows, and of artifice and industry, which were attributes Walker used in extolling the New York Book-Bindery.[11]

Another typical Walker binding is the one for the first edition of Lossing's *Seventeen Hundred and Seventy-Six* (1847), shown in figures 4a and 4b.[12] It is more intricate than that of *The Art of Book-Binding* and is an especially revealing example of Walker's tastes and aims. The major elements of the design can be divided into four categories. The first category can be called "traditional design," as present in the large frame blocked in blind on the upper cover. It resembles stylized medieval tracery, and many of its details, like foliation, grotesques, and drapings, may have been the kind of decoration Walker thought was inappropriate or stale (fig. 4a). The second category includes "conventional symbols or emblems" based on either classical or Christian traditions. The star and cherubs blowing horns at the head of the spine fall into this group (fig. 4b). The third category, which may be called "realistic emblems," as opposed to traditional emblems, are more closely indicative of a particular time, as exemplified by the Minute Man on the spine who is calling the farmer to arms (fig. 4b). The fourth category is "pictorial representation" of historic persons, like Washington and Franklin, or historic events, as in the scene in the center of the cover showing Washington receiving his commission as Commander-in-Chief of the Continental Army.

Walker's arrangement of the elements that compose the binding's design thus comes close to being a hierarchy of ornamentation, one that moves from the universal to the specific or from the timeless to the historical. This is not to imply that the decorations in the different categories are unrelated to one another. On the contrary, they are executed to form an integrated, unified design: the blind frame, for instance, "supports" and draws one's eye toward the central scene in gold. These interrelationships are duplicated in several minor ways. The medallion of Franklin, for instance, is supported by two American figures, an Indian on the left and a Revolutionary soldier on the right (fig. 4a). Another instance may be seen in the draping at the top left and right of the cover. Though the use of draping as a decorative motif in binding dates from centuries past, the embossing found in each example here is typically American. The left piece has the Tree of Liberty and the legend Liberty; the right piece has a coiled snake and the motto Don't Tread On Me (fig. 4a). Our response to the binding, therefore, is a fluid one, moving from the general to the specific and from the abstract to the historical.

The scene on the upper cover of the book is singularly apt because it depicts an actual historic event from the American Revolution of 1776. On the remote chance that the viewer or reader might not recognize the scene, Walker has labeled it "Washington Receiving His Commission."[13] In producing this decoration Walker adhered closely to the principle of "appropriateness" that Joseph Cundall (1818–1895) advocated and with which Walker agreed: "One of the principles which I would seek to establish in Ornamental Art in Bookbinding is, that every book should be decorated as far as possible in accordance with its contents" [3, p. 13].[14]

Even though all the elements of the design combine to make a single statement, some viewers might complain that there is simply too much, that the binding is too "busy." Is there perhaps a lack of discipline? Is it "appropriate" to use five different styles of nineteenth-century display type on a book's spine? Such questions can only be answered when more of Walker's bindings are examined. And even though he may be criticized for excessive ornamentation on his bindings or for borrowing many of his ideas and descriptions about binding from earlier writers, Walker should also be applauded for his efforts at promoting contemporary binding styles using American motifs. The enthusiasm for binding that is evident everywhere in *The Art of Book-Binding* was not meant only to drum up new business, but was also a reflection of Walker's deep interest in bookbinding—ideas and feelings that often were manifested in the bindings from the New York Book-Bindery, legacies still to be discovered and appreciated.

Paul S. Koda
Chapel Hill

Appendix

Although Walker's main business was his commercial bindery, it should be stressed that publishing became an important part of his life and of the life of the bindery. His active publishing years were between the early 1840s and the middle 1870s, when the bindery was located on Fulton Street (it moved to Dey Street in 1871). Before Walker got into full-scale book publishing there may have been an intermediate step between binding and publishing. The advertisement for the new store on 114 Fulton Street, which developed from the bindery at 112 Fulton, only included the services of "Bookbinding, Bookselling, and Stationery," not publishing [27]. As a bookseller Walker had close business ties with Robert Sears, in that the store was "the Depot for Sears' Popular Pictorial Works"; these ties were further strengthened through bookbinding in that Walker sold Sears' *Illustrations of the Bible,* Sears' *Bible Biography,* and Sears' *Wonders of the World* in "Richly Ornamented Bindings" [27].

In later years Walker occupied several other publishing offices, which were probably rented when the publishing business improved. In 1845, for example, he was publishing books from 128 Nassau [6], a location he seems to have occupied for only a year, after which the city directory lists only the Fulton Street address. In 1853 he expanded to 54 Gold [25]; in 1864 he was at 38 Walker; in 1874 he rejoined the bindery at 55 Dey. For at least one period Walker expanded the publishing side of the business outside the city of New York. In an advertisement for his publications at the end of John Dowling's *Life and Reign of Pope Pius the Ninth* (1849) he lists a Philadelphia address: No. 41, South Fourth Street [7]. And toward the end of his life Walker had another firm distribute his books; *The American Catalogue* for 1876 states that his publications could only be obtained "care [of] C. H. Jones & Co. 114 Fulton St." [1, p. 21]. (Walker still owned the building but had rented it to Jones.) He also had invested in another publishing company; his will bequeathed to his children and grandchildren "two hundred and ninety-five shares of the stock and property now standing in my name, and owned by me in the 'Leonard Scott Publishing Company' " [29].

Early in his publishing career Walker collaborated with other publishers and authors in order to publish books. It may have been the way he started as a publisher, and his earliest collaboration may well have been with Robert Sears, with whom he co-published several books in 1844. Some of those 1844 publications include *A New and Complete History of the Holy Bible, The Wonders of the World,* and *Bible Biography.* Sears probably whetted Walker's interest in illustrated books. Along those lines Walker's most fruitful collaboration seems to have been with Benson J. Lossing, about whom Walker says in the Publisher's Notice to *Seventeen Hundred and Seventy-Six*: "Having experienced the skill of Mr. Lossing (of the firm of Lossing & Barritt, engravers) in the illustration of 'Dowling's History of Romanism,' and other works, and having full confidence in his ability as a writer, I have intrusted to him both the authorship of this volume and its pictorial embellishment" [16, p. v]. Lossing and Walker also worked together on publications for children. In 1850 they issued *The Juvenile Odd-Fellow,* a collection of pious writings for children edited by P. G. Paschal Donaldson (fl. 1850). They also produced a short-lived periodical for children, the *Young People's Mirror* (1848–1849). (The appearance of the interior view of the Westleys and Clark's bindery—which Walker later used for the frontispiece of *The Art of Book-Binding*—in an advertisement in the *Young People's Mirror,* fig. 3 above, makes one wonder whether it might have been Lossing, or a member of his firm, who copied the wood engravings from Knight.) After 1850 Lossing began to use other publishers, but it was his early relationship with Walker that helped him to launch his successful career.

John Dowling's (1807–1878) *History of Romanism,* through which Walker had become impressed with Lossing's work, turned out to be Walker's most popular publication. It first appeared in 1845, and by 1849 had reached a seventeenth edition. The book was published as late as 1871 and was the only copyright mentioned and bequeathed in Walker's will [29].

These are only a few of the titles that Walker published, yet in many ways they are representative. For the most part they are "safe" books, ones that guaranteed a predictable number of sales. They appealed to an identifiable readership and attitude, like the sentimental poems in the Odd Fellows' book *Friendship, Love and Truth* (1849), or were tried-and-true literature like the *Arabian Nights* (1844), patriotic compilations like Edwin Williams's (1797–1854) *Statesman's Manual* (1854), or useful reference works like Kemble's map of the city of New York (1846).

The most popular of Walker's sentimental publications was *The Odd-Fellows Offering*, which appealed both to the popular imagination as well as to an identifiable buying public. Between 1848 and 1854 Walker published seven of the twelve issues of the *Offering* [9, p. 56]. (It originally appeared in 1843, and its run was one of the longest for an American literary annual at a time when most of them were published for only a single year; additional information about the *Offering* appears in Faxon [9], Kirkham and Fink [12], and Thompson [23].)

As with *The Art of Book-Binding*, Walker was not timid about borrowing literary material for his annuals. It was common practice: Faxon points out that "*The Wreath of Wild Flowers*, a book of miscellanies, by John Milton Stearns [1810–1898], published in New York in 1846" was reissued over several years by different firms and was "used without credit by the publishers" [9, pp. xix, 76]. The publisher of the original edition in 1846 was Walker himself.

That Walker wanted to be in the mainstream of popular publishing is further emphasized by his ready adoption (again from England) of the immensely successful publishing themes and techniques of Charles Knight (1791–1873) and the Society for the Diffusion of Useful Knowledge. He used Knight's motto, Knowledge is Power, and adapted the Society's name in an advertisement (in Dowling's *Pius the Ninth* [7]) describing his own publishing firm, which he elaborately called the "American National and Pictorial Book Establishment, for the Diffusion of Useful Knowledge Among the People," announcing further that "the Public are assured that no books of an Ephemeral or Demoralizing character will be issued from this Establishment: it is the Proprietor's highest pleasure to publish only such Books as will dignify and improve the Reader."

Even though Walker was active in publishing for many years, he did not become a major publisher. He may not have had the financial resources or the talent or the time to run the publishing side of his business as a steady commercial venture.

Bibliographical Note

Fold collation: [1]⁶, X1, 2⁸, 2★⁸, [3]⁸.

Page collation: [i–ii blank]; ²[i blank, ii–iii, iv blank, v, vi blank, vii] viii; 13–49; [50 blank]; 51–64.

Signed: '2' on 2-5ʳ; '2★' on 2-1ʳ.

Paper: Machine-made wove; leaf 2-1 measures 21.4 x 13.9 x .013 cm; preliminaries, text, and subsidiaries bulk at .39 cm.

Binding: Cased in crimson morocco-grained cloth; three-line border blocked in blind on upper and lower covers; floriated gilt frame and title stamped in gold on upper cover, identical frame with central floral bouquet in blind on lower cover; all edges gilt; pale yellow machine-made endpapers (see fig. 1).

Note: Other copies of the book have been seen in dark green cloth.

Notes

1. Our chief source of information on Walker's changing business circumstances is the annual city directories of New York [6, 15, 25]. Unless otherwise specified in reference brackets, the dates mentioned in adjacent text will lead the reader to the appropriate volumes. Because information in nineteenth-century directories is often incomplete, inaccurate, or obsolete, the dates of Walker's activities may have to be revised in light of future research.

2. Although Joseph brought the suit against his father's will, James is mentioned as the problem child. Contesting the will probably had less to do with family feelings than with who gained the most from the inheritance. Walker had five children in all.

3. S. T. Prideaux calls the book "an advertisement for E. Walker's Bookbindery" [20, p. 292].

4. The corresponding pages between *The Art of Book-Binding* and its sources are as follows:

Source	Walker's Page(s)	Sources' Page(s)
Arnett [2]	24	4–5
"	25	69, 12
"	26	23
Cundall [3]	27–30	4–8
Knight [13]	30–37	378–84
Arnett	38	121
"	39	49
"	40	51, 126 ff.

5. Knight may not have been the author of the article on bookbinding, because it was reprinted in an 1843 collection of essays called *Days at the Factories* [5, pp. 362–84]. The author listed on the title page is George Dodd (1808–1881), who was Knight's editorial assistant. (Also see Wakeman [26, p. 15] on Knight and Dodd.) Walker knew about the article as early as 1843, because

it was reprinted with the title "A Day at a Bookbindery," in Robert Sears' *New Monthly Family Magazine* [4]. The article concludes with an acknowledgment to Walker for the information about bookbinding that he provided and with a tribute to the moral climate in his bindery:

> It remains only for us to acknowledge the courtesy of Mr. E. Walker, of this city, who has furnished us with many particulars in this brief sketch; and we can not conclude without again bearing testimony to the excellent moral effects that the manner in which his establishment is conducted produces upon the persons of both sexes who are in his employ. [4, p. 207]

The publisher of the magazine was Robert Sears (1810–1892), who was a recognized publisher of periodicals and illustrated books in the nineteenth century. He was "also one of the earliest of the New York publishers to make a serious effort to serve the nation as a whole, without regard to sectional differences" (*DNB* 8:541), which is borne out by the copy of the issue just quoted from, in that it was co-published by William Richards (fl. 1840s), who was Sears' co-editor, in Penfield, Georgia. Along with the readers who read the bookbinding article in *The Penny Magazine* there were many others who learned about nineteenth-century bookbinding from Sears' magazine. It is also worth noting that the *DNB* article on Sears says that between "1844 and 1849 he edited and published under various titles a magazine, finally known as the *New Pictorial Family Magazine*." The existence of the *New Monthly Family Magazine* shows that publication of Sears' periodical began as early as January 1843.

6. It is confusing to have the same name for the two kinds of presses. The probable historic reason for this is that both produced raised designs, even though their construction and operation differed. Cloth from a continuous roll was embossed by passing it between two revolving metal cylinders, much like the drying apparatus on old-fashioned washing machines. It produced a repeating pattern. The cloth was cut to fit books of every size. The other kind of embossing was usually done after

the covering material had been glued to the boards. In this operation the design was pressed into the cover by the up-and-down movement of a horizontal die. In special instances it was called embossing (see Jamieson [10]), but it was also called stamping or blocking. This kind of work was also done on an arming press. The decorations were designed to fit specific books. Interestingly, Sears' illustration of the press (see note 5 above) is the same as Walker's, not Knight's. Sears calls the press both an "embossing-press" and an "embossing-machine" [4, p. 206].

7. Both Walker and Knight were obviously impressed with the size, force, and cost of these machines. These presses (especially when powered hydraulically) were the kinds of machines typically manufactured in the Industrial Revolution. Except for the adoption of cloth as a cover for books, no other development had a greater impact on the design and production of bookbindings in the first half of the nineteenth century. More information about these presses is in Arnett [2], Ellenport [8], Faxon [9], Jamieson [10], and Johnson [11].

8. Lossing was in partnership with William Barritt (b. ca. 1822); they were mainly engravers, but Lossing expanded his career as a popular writer of American history.

9. Other binding styles that were available from the New York Book-Bindery are listed on pp. 48–49 and in the advertisements on pp. 51–64.

10. Walker may have come to his distrust of Jones's standards of taste and design through the writings of Joseph Cundall. For a brief discussion of Cundall's attitude toward Jones see McLean [17, pp. 15–16].

11. The bee motif was not an uncommon embellishment on nineteenth-century books about industry and manufacturing. The upper and lower covers of Samuel Timmins's *Industrial History of Birmingham* [24], for example, have vertical rows of bees blocked in blind. Beehives are featured in the Mormons' Deseret publications. Bees and beekeeping also figure strongly in classical literature (Aristotle, Varro, Columella, and especially Virgil's *Georgics* 4).

12. Walker seems to have signed only the bindings of books that he published, and not always those. The only location he appears to have put his name was at the tail of a book's spine (see fig. 4b).

13. It is interesting to note that the scene on the upper cover of an 1850 issue of the book is different. Walker used instead a reproduction of John Trumbull's (1756–1843) famous painting, usually called *The Declaration of Independence, July 4, 1776,* but which more accurately shows the presentation of the Declaration to the Continental Congress. As more of Walker's bindings are identified and recorded it may be possible to determine whether the Trumbull illustration was simply an alternative binding choice or whether Walker thought it was a more recognizable and, therefore, an even more appropriate binding illustration for the book.

14. Walker also talks (p. 25) about the appropriateness of certain binding leathers and colors for different kinds of writing. Although he quotes Thomas Frognall Dibdin (1776–1847) as the source for his ideas, he more than likely got them from Arnett [2, pp. 69–71], who quotes Dibdin. Wakeman [26] also has an excellent discussion of every aspect of nineteenth-century trade bindings and binding practices.

References

1. *The American Catalogue, July 1, 1876.* New York: A. C. Armstrong, 1880.
2. Arnett, John Andrews. *Bibliopegia; or, The Art of Bookbinding.* 1835. Reprint. New York: Garland, 1980.
3. Cundall, Joseph. *On Ornamental Art, Applied to Ancient and Modern Bookbinding.* [London]: Society of Arts, 1848.
4. "A Day at a Bookbindery." In *Sears' New Monthly Family Magazine.* 1:5 (May 1843): 200-207.
5. Dodd, George. *Days at the Factories; or, the Manufacturing Industry of Great Britain Described.* London: Charles Knight, 1843. Reprint. New York: Augustus M. Kelley, 1967.
6. *Doggett's New-York City Directory.* New York: John Doggett, Jr., 1842–1851.
7. Dowling, John. *The Life and Reign of Pope Pius the Ninth.* New York: Edward Walker, 1849.
8. Ellenport, Samuel B. *An Essay on the Development & Usage of Brass Plate Dies.* Boston: Harcourt Bindery, 1980.
9. Faxon, Frederick Winthrop. *Literary Annuals and Gift-Books.* Boston: Boston Book Company, 1912. Reprint. Pinner: Private Libraries Association, 1973.
10. Jamieson, Eleanore. *English Embossed Bindings 1825-1850.* Cambridge: Cambridge University Press, 1972.
11. Johnson, Mary-Parke. "An Inventory of Machinery, Tools, Materials, Stock and Unfinished Work at the Joseph T. Altemus Bookbindery." Master's thesis, University of North Carolina at Chapel Hill, 1982.
12. Kirkham, E. Bruce, and John W. Fink, comps. *Indices to "American Literary Annuals and Gift Books 1825-1865."* New Haven: Research Publications, 1975.
13. Knight, Charles. "A Day at a Bookbinders." *The Penny Magazine.* Suppl. 11 (September 1842): 377–84.
14. London. Great Exhibition of the Works of Industry of All

Nations, 1851. *Official Descriptive and Illustrated Catalogue.*
London: Spicer Brothers, 1851.

15. *Longworth's American Almanac, New-York Register, and City Directory.* New York: Thomas Longworth, 1835–1842.

16. Lossing, Benson J. *Seventeen Hundred and Seventy-Six; or, The War of Independence.* New York: Edward Walker, 1847.

17. McLean, Ruari. *Victorian Publishers' Book-Bindings in Cloth and Leather.* Berkeley and Los Angeles: University of California Press, 1973.

18. *The New York Mercantile Register, for 1847–48, Containing the Cards of the Principal Business Establishments . . . in New York City.* New York: George F. Nesbitt, 1847.

19. *New York Times,* 24 January 1852, 1:4.

20. Prideaux, S. T. *An Historical Sketch of Bookbinding.* London: Lawrence & Bullen, 1893.

21. Ramsden, Charles. *London Bookbinders: 1780–1840.* London: B. T. Batsford, 1956.

22. "Report of the Commissioners." In *The Illustrated Exhibitor, A Tribute to the World's Industrial Jubilee,* v–vi. London: John Cassell, 1851.

23. Thompson, Ralph. *American Literary Annuals & Gift Books, 1825–1865.* New York: H. W. Wilson, 1936.

24. Timmins, Samuel. *The Resources, Products, and Industrial History of Birmingham and the Midland Hardware District.* London: Robert Hardwicke, 1866.

25. *Trow's New-York City Directory.* New York: John F. Trow, 1853–1894.

26. Wakeman, Geoffrey. *Nineteenth Century Trade Binding.* Oxford: The Plough Press, 1983.

27. [Walker, Edward]. Advertisement. *Sears' New Monthly Family Magazine* 1:5 (May 1843): verso of upper wrapper of Penfield, Georgia, issue, published by William Richards.

28. [Walker, Edward]. Certificate of Death (1879:146). Vital Records, City Hall, Yonkers, New York. Photocopy.

29. Walker, Edward. Last Will and Testament, 22 September 1877. Surrogate's Office, Westchester County, New York. Photocopy.

30. [Walker, Edward]. Obituary. *New-York Daily* [*Herald*] *Tribune*, 13 January 1879, 2:6.

31. [Walker, Edward]. Obituary. *New York Times*, 13 January 1879, 5:4.

32. Walker, Edward. "The Publisher's Address to His Brethren." In *The Odd-Fellows' Offering for 1853*, 5–6. New York: Edward Walker, 1852.

33. Walker, Emily. Deposition, 7 March 1879. Walker Papers, 1879:338. Surrogate's Court, Westchester County, New York. Photocopy.

34. Walker, Sophia A. S. S. Deposition, 8 March 1879. Walker Papers, 1879:338. Surrogate's Court, Westchester County, New York. Photocopy.

35. *Young People's Mirror*. New York: Edward Walker, 1848–1849.

The Art of Book-Binding

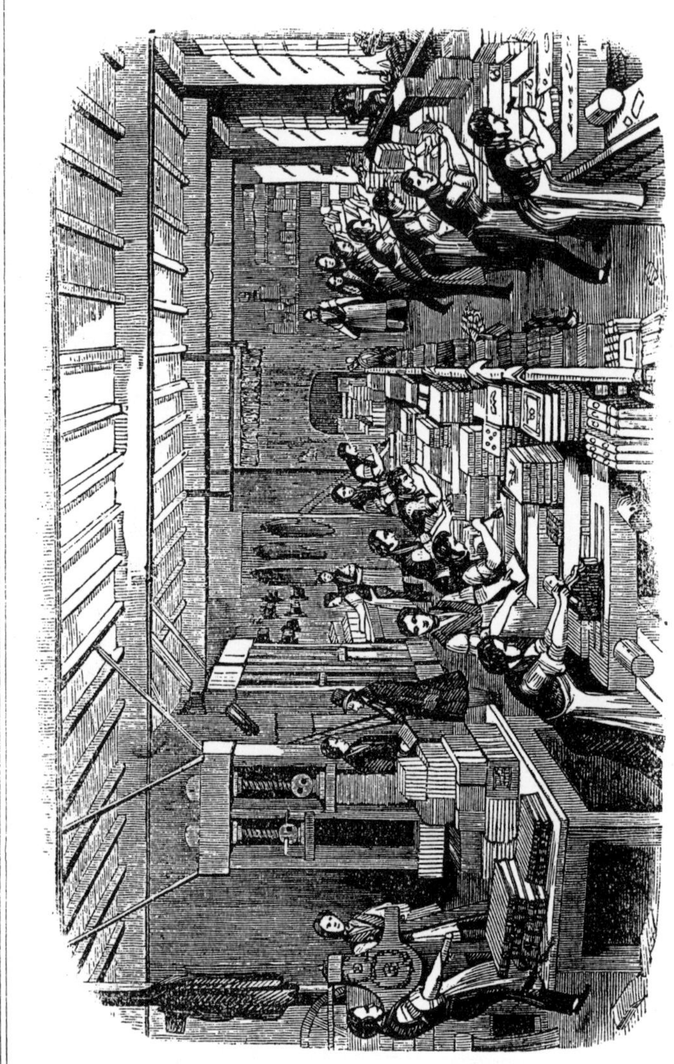

THE NEW YORK BOOK-BINDERY

THE

ART OF BOOK-BINDING,

ITS RISE AND PROGRESS;

INCLUDING

A DESCRIPTIVE ACCOUNT OF THE

NEW YORK BOOK-BINDERY.

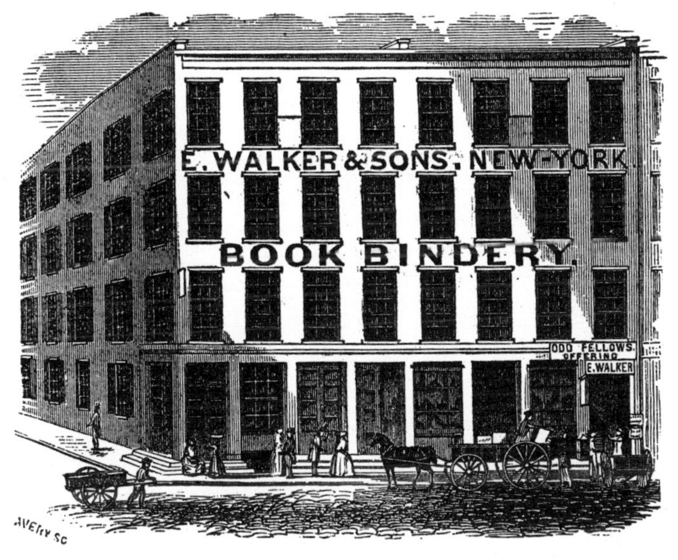

NEW YORK:
E. WALKER & SONS, 114 FULTON STREET.

1850.

" How I love Books,
not only for the imaginative
pleasures they afford me, but
for their making me love to be in
contact with them. I look sideways
at my *Spenser*, my *Theocritus*, and my
Arabian Nights; then on my left side
at my *Chaucer*; and think how natural it was for Charles Lamb to give a
kiss to an old folio, as I once saw him
do to *Chapman's Homer*. Nothing,
while I live and think, can deprive
me of my value of such treasures.
I can help the appreciation of
them while I last, and love
them till I die."
Leigh Hunt.

THIS little manual, descriptive of the origin and progress of book-binding, has been prepared by the publisher, expressly for the use of his numerous patrons, in the belief that it will be found to comprise much curious and interesting matter relative to the bibliopegistic art, which will prove acceptable to all true lovers of books. "Books," says Milton, "are among the sweetest luxuries of our world;" and Channing affirms that "in the best books, great men talk to us, with us, and give us their most precious thoughts. Books are the voices of the distant and the dead. Books are the true levellers. They give to all who will faithfully use them the society and the presence of the best and greatest of our race. No matter how poor I am; no matter though the prosperous of my own time will not enter my obscure dwelling. If learned men and poets will enter and take up their abode under my roof—if Milton will cross my threshold to sing to me of Paradise; and Shakspeare open to me the worlds of imagination, and the workings of the human heart; and Franklin enrich me with his practical wisdom—I shall not pine for want of intellectual companionship, and I may become a cultivated man, though excluded from what is called the best society in the place where I live." Books have in all ages commanded the veneration of mankind; and this appreciation of their value has been commonly evinced by the skill and ingenuity devoted to their decoration. Nor is this devotion to the internal and external adornment of books peculiar to past ages; it is no less a characteristic of our own, when the resources of taste and inventive art have become well nigh exhausted in the lavish expenditure of costly embellishment which distinguishes many of our modern literary productions. There are, however, exceptions to the rule.

Good books, it has been well observed, deserve good binding; did they but contain the power of speech, as well as all manner of tongues, how many tales of woe would they relate to us of the neglect and destruction they have suffered, merely for the want of a decent covering, which would have secured to them the friendship and esteem of the scholar, as well as universal admiration.

ART OF BOOK-BINDING

AVERY. Sc

The art and mystery of book-binding, from its connexion with the progress of literary enterprise, necessarily possesses a peculiar interest and importance in the world of letters.   A few brief notices of the early scribes, illuminators, and publishers, may not therefore be deemed inappropriate, as introductory to the following sketch of the book-binding art.

13

The literary profession originated even in classic times, when an extensive traffic was carried on in MSS., by the Scribes and Copyists; it also flourished during the Saxon era, many eminent names being on record of transcribers in the seventh and eighth centuries. Books in their present form were invented, it is said, by Attalus, King of Pergamus, in 887.

The diffusive spread of knowledge, and the founding of monasteries, gave increased importance to this branch of commerce, although the earliest mention of a "public dealer in books" is of one Peter de Blois, who lived about 1170. He was a distinguished scholar, having been remarkable for his great erudition.

Bibliopoles of the olden time exercised their calling under the supervision and censorship of the Universities; and books were then, moreover, rare and costly luxuries—the prerogative of the privileged few; now they have become the common property of mankind.

During the middle ages, the booksellers were called *Stationarii* at the Universities of Paris and Bologna; but the first regularly matriculated bookseller was doubtless Faustus, for he is said to have carried his books for sale to the Monasteries in France, and elsewhere. The first bookseller who purchased MSS. for publication, and speculated in the enterprise (not possessing a press of his own), was John Otto, of Nuremberg, who flourished in 1516. Caxton, the father of the English press, however, who lived 1471–1491, and who had twenty-four presses in his office at Westminster Abbey, doubtless issued many new and original productions at his own risk, as well as older works, and the emanations of his own pen.

The history of the publishing business, from the invention of the " divine art" to the close of the seventeenth century, is graced with a luminous train of illustrious names, as author-booksellers, whose literary attainments and critical acumen shed lustre alike on both the pursuits of author and publisher.

From the days of Caxton to the accession of James I., the press appears to have been to no inconsiderable extent devoted to the printing of classical works; this preference for the literary stores of antiquity, however, was not restricted to the English press, it prevailed to a still greater degree among the printers of Germany, Italy, and France. The labors of the Alduses, the Stephenses, and the Plantins, were thus consecrated, till at the dawn, and during the era of the Reformation, the printing of the Sacred Scriptures, in a great measure, divided the attention of the printers. The celebrated names of Wynkin de Worde, Pynson, Weir, Day, Dunton, Tonson, Lintot, and Ballard, with others, form a luminous train of illustrious bibliopoles, whose literary enterprises occupy a conspicuous feature in early literary history, for some of them contributed in no small degree to enrich numerically the estate of English literature—Wynkin de Worde, the able associate and successor of Caxton, having printed four hundred and eight distinct works, while Pynson, Day, and others, issued more than half that number, each. Between the years 1474 and 1600, it has been estimated about 350 printers flourished in England and Scotland, and that the products of their several presses amounted in the aggregate to 10,000 distinct productions. At the great fire of London in 1666, the booksellers of Paternoster Row sustained a serious loss—as heavy a calamity to them, as the destruction of the Alexandrian Library was to the ancients. Dwelling in such close proximity to St. Paul's, they were accustomed to deposit large quantities of books, for their supposed greater safety, in the vaults of the Old Cathedral; these, at the time of the fire, were valued by Evelyn at £200,000.

In ancient times, a great variety of materials were used in making books; plates of lead and copper, bricks, wooden planks, and the thin part of the bark of the lime, ash, and maple. From hence is derived the term *liber*, which signifies the inner bark of trees; and as these were rolled up to render them portable, they were called *volumen*, or volume—a name afterwards given to the like rolls of papyrus, parchment, and paper. The two earliest works of which we have any knowledge are the Pentateuch and the Iliad— one being part of a divine revelation, and the other one of the greatest achievements of human genius.

Josephus speaks of two columns—the one of stone, the other of brick,—on which the children of Seth wrote their inventions and astronomical discoveries. Writing, according to the same authority, was invented by Seth. Porphyry makes mention of some pillars, preserved in Crete, on which the ceremonies practised by the Corybantes in their sacrifices were recorded. Hesiod's works were originally written upon tables of lead, and deposited in the Temple of the Muses in Bœotia. The Ten Commandments delivered to Moses, we are informed in Holy Writ, were written upon stone; and Solon's laws were recorded upon wooden planks. Tables of wood, box, and ivory were commonly used for the purpose among the ancients: when of wood, they were frequently covered with wax, to render the surface easier for inscribing. The art of making paper from fibrous matter, reduced to a pulp in water, which is the present method, appears to have been invented by the Chinese about the year 95 A.D. Previously to this time, the inner bark of the bamboo was used, and a style or bodkin then supplied the place of the pen. Before the invention of paper from cotton, which occurred about the year 1000 of the Christian era, the Egyptian *papyrus*, from which the term paper is derived, was the material principally used for writing purposes. The papyrus consisted of thin consecutive coats, or pellicles, that surround the stock of this reedy plant; the slips were laid out to dry, and then polished for use. Papyrus was a great article of commerce in the East; it was used, indeed, throughout Europe, and extensively at Rome. Among other works, the New Testament was originally written upon this fabric. Numerous specimens of ancient writings upon papyrus are still extant; some Greek MSS., supposed to have been written about the year 135 B.C., some Egyptian MSS. at Leyden, and others at the Vatican, of as remote a date as 646 years B.C. Vast numbers were discovered among the ruins of Herculaneum. Parchment, usually made of the skins of sheep, derives its name from Pergamus, where it is said to have been invented by Eumenes, about 197 B.C., in consequence of the scarcity of the papyrus. To such delicate texture was it susceptible of being brought, that Cicero is said to have seen a copy of the *Iliad* transcribed so minutely upon it, as to be placed within a nut-shell. Multitudes of valuable MSS. were destroyed in Italy and other parts of southern Europe during the 5th century, and for nearly a thousand years literature was little cultivated in Europe. A few monks and others occupied themselves with transcribing the more celebrated productions, and many of these caligraphists attained to great skill in their art. Thus the Scriptures were handed down to our times, as well as most of the Greek and Roman classics; and we have to thank those religious ascetics for the preservation of most of our literary treasures.

So precious were manuscripts in those days, that an Anglo-Saxon bishop, named Wilfred, had the books of the four evangelists copied out in letters of gold upon purple parchment; and such value did he set upon the work when it was completed, that he kept it in a case of gold adorned with precious stones. Few men, excepting the monks, were capable of writing in those early times. We find a certain king of Kent, affixing to a charter the sign of a cross, and causing the scribe to add below, that it was on account of his ignorance of writing that he could not sign his name.

Prior to the invention of printing, as books were multiplied by the slow process of transcribing, during the middle ages, this task was performed by monks aud illuminators with singular devotion, for they sometimes were occupied for years in the writing and embellishment of these productions. Books in those days were few indeed, as well as readers, but the process was laborious in the extreme, compared with the present times. Nor are the attractions of genius alone deemed sufficient to satisfy the taste of the age ; the choicest resources of decorative art are put in requisition for the internal and external embellishment of the several products of the mind. In the middle ages, even bishops and monks loved to engage in the art of book-binding. Reference is made to the fact by Bede, who cites an instance of a superbly illuminated Prayer-book, the binding of which was of pure ivory, studded with gems. There were also trading binders, called *Ligatores.*

Our forefathers used to exhibit the leaves instead of the backs of their books, being ambitious of displaying the silken strings and gold or silver clasps. The art of ornamenting the exterior was carried to a lavish extent; jewels as well as precious metals, were employed to evince their splendor.

Peacham advises as follows:—" Have a care of keeping your books handsome and well bound, not casting away over much in their gilding and stringing, for ostentation sake,—like the prayer bokes of girles and gallants, which are carried to church for their outsides."

There are many instances upon record of sumptuous bindings ; some specimens of missals are still extant, with covers of solid silver, gilt. Gold, relics, ivory, velvet, large bosses of brass, and other costly ornaments, were formerly used for the exterior decoration of books. Queen Elizabeth was very choice over a little tome, the composition of Catharine Parr, which was inclosed in a solid gold cover, and which she used to carry about with her as a " pet book," attached to her side by a golden chain. The manuscript copy of the Gospels, used originally at the Coronation of Henry I., and down to that of Edward VI., which is said to be still extant, is of a different description, being inclosed within oaken boards, an inch thick, fastened together with thongs of leather and brass bosses—a dainty object for kingly lips to kiss, in token of their submission to their coronation oath. This book was literally bound in *boards*.

Illuminated books were in much repute from the sixth to the seventeenth century. A monk was employed thirty years in the monastery of St. Audeon, on one missal. It was finished 1682.

Many of the manuscripts of the mediæval age were magnificent in the extreme; sometimes they were inscribed with liquid gold on parchment of the richest purple, and adorned with brilliant illuminations of exquisite workmanship. All this prodigal decoration, however, tended greatly to enhance the price of books to an extent which to us would sound enormously extravagant. Thanks to the invention of "the divine art" and the agency of steam, we now may multiply books to an almost unlimited extent, and at an incredibly trifling expense. The rich and elaborate illuminations of the laborious monks and scribes of olden times we also re-produce in all their gorgeousness and splendor, at almost a fraction of their original cost. The same remark applies with equal force to the external decorations in binding of books; the most exquisite skill having been evinced in the emblematic devices lavished upon them.

Book-binding has been deemed one of the most difficult arts; it is incontestably one requiring no little care, neatness, taste, and skill, as may be easily seen in the three great characteristics of good binding,—solidity, elasticity, and elegance. This will be also evinced in the various processes of coloring and preparing the leather, the curious and ingenious devices for decorating the covers, and marbling or gilding the edges of books. *Forwarding* has ever been deemed the great desideratum of all good binding. The early binders were very rigid upon this point, as may be seen by the following extract from the Code of laws of 1750, referring to this particular. "Be it held, that the master binders do sew all their books with thread and real bands, do back them with parchment, and not paper; and in case of infringement the said books shall be done again at the expense of the infringer; who shall besides be condemned to a fine of thirty pounds for each volume." Care in this respect is of the utmost importance, when the book is valuable, either from its rarity or the splendor of its embellishment, such works daily augmenting in price; for if carelessly or badly bound, the re-binding, and consequent cropping the book down by re-cutting the edges, tends considerably to depreciate its value,—a good margin being "a primary object with the genuine book collector."

Dr. Dibdin, who, from his long and intimate connexion with the most celebrated book collectors of Europe, may be regarded as no mean authority, in speaking of book-binding, thus pleads its claims. "The general appearance of one's library is by no means a matter of mere foppery or indifference; it is a sort of cardinal point to which the tasteful collector does well to take heed. You have a right to consider books as to their *outsides*,—with the eye of a painter; because this does not militate against the proper use of the contents." This learned pundit recommends *russia* for works on antiquity, architecture, or history, and light colored calf for works in belles-lettres.

Particular departments of literature have their respective kinds of binding.; for example, theological works are usually bound in dark blue,

2

purple, black, or some sedate color. Law books have their established livery, known as law binding, the leather being left its natural color, light brown or fawn color; and the edges of the leaves white. Dutch binding is where the backs are of vellum or parchment. Some collectors have adopted a peculiar livery for the binding of their entire libraries—sometimes half calf or half morocco, gilt. The styles of binding for the various classes of literature are designated by the terms, *filleted, lettered gilt, half extra, super extra,* according to the quality and style of ornament bestowed upon a book. Stationery or blank book binding is also another distinct branch of the art.

"It is yet with books," says Hume, "as with women, where a certain plainness of dress and style is more engaging than that glare of paint and apparel, which so dazzle the eye, but reach not the affections;" although it cannot be denied that most are delighted with an elegantly bound book. The casket should be worthy of the gem it incloses; or, as Shakspeare says,

> "A book in many's eyes doth share the glory
> That in gold clasps locks in the golden story."

When the art of book-binding was first invented, it is impossible to ascertain. Phillatius, a learned Athenian, was the first who pointed out the use of a particular glue for fastening the leaves of a book together—an invention which his countrymen thought of such importance, that they erected a statue to his memory. The most ancient mode of binding consisted in glueing the different leaves together, and attaching them to cylinders of wood, round which they were rolled: this is called Egyptian binding, and continued to be practised long after the age of Augustus. This method is yet in use in oriental countries, and in Jewish synagogues, where they still continue to write books of the law on strips of vellum sewed together, so as to form only one long page; on each extremity of which is a roller, furnished with clasps of gold or silver.

The Romans carried the art of book-binding to a considerable perfection; and some of their public officers had books called Diptychs, in which their acts were written. An old writer says that about the Christian era the books of the Romans were covered with red, yellow, green, and purple leather, and decorated with silver and gold. In the 13th century, some of the Gospels, missals, and service books for the use of the Greek and Roman churches were covered in gold and silver; some were also enamelled and enriched with precious stones and pearls of great value.

In the 15th century, when Art was universal, such men as Albert Durer, Raffaelle, and Giulio Romano decorated books. The use of calf and morocco binding seems to have followed the introduction of printing; and there are many printed books bound in calf with oaken boards. About the 15th and beginning of the 16th centuries they were stamped with gold and blind tools. The earliest of these tools generally represent figures, such as Christ, St. Paul, coats of arms, &c.,—according to the contents of the book.

In the reign of Henry VIII., about 1538, Grafton the printer undertook to print the Great Bible; for which purpose he went to Paris, there not being sufficient men or types in England. He had not, however, proceeded far before he was stopped in the progress of this heretical book; when he returned to England, bringing with him presses, type, printers, and book-binders, and finished the work in 1539. Henry VIII. had many books bound in velvet, with gold bosses and ornaments; and in his reign the stamping of tools in gold appears to have been introduced. In the reign of Queen Elizabeth some exquisite bindings were done by embroidery. The Queen herself used to work the covers with gold and silver thread, spangles, &c. Count Grolier seems to have been a great patron of the art on the continent; and all his books were bound in smooth morocco or calf, ornamented with gold.

The style of the books of Maioli was very similar to that of Grolier, or those of Diana of Poictiers—the specimens done for her being among the finest ever produced, and were no doubt designed by Petit Bernard. Roger Paine was the first Englishman who produced a really good binding; and some of his best works, such as French romances, were powdered with the fleur-de-lis. His books on chivalry had suitable ornaments; on poetical works he used a simple lyre; and he carried the emblematical style of binding as far as emblems ought to be used.

The bibliopegist is as essential as the typographer and the author, to the production of an elegant book; and the mechanic skill of the two former, no less than the genius of the author, deserves an appropriate recognition.

The various mechanical details and social economy of an extensive book-bindery like that referred to in the following pages, which is the oldest establishment of its class in New York, cannot, it is believed, prove altogether uninteresting to the lovers of literature and the public generally.

The principal warehouse (for a sketch of which, see frontispiece) is where the operations are conducted for binding books in cloth boards, the most prevalent style at the present day. In one department, females are engaged in folding the sheets, gathering them into groups, sewing them into the form of a book, &c.; while in this room are men pursuing the subsequent operations of glueing, pasting, cutting, hammering, pressing, &c., by which the book is brought to a finished state. This is a very busy scene, and one presenting much variety, from the distinct nature of the processes carried on.

Book-binding, as already intimated, requires the exercise of great care, dexterity, and taste, as well as laborious devotion to its several details, in order to insure success. There are separate and distinct branches of the business,—plain and ornamental book-binding, law binding, and blank book and ledger binding. The latter is a department in itself, and is usually conducted by stationers.

The various sizes of books, it is known, are designated by the number of leaves in which the sheet is folded. For instance, folio is two leaf, quarto, four leaves, octavo, eight, duodecimo, twelve to a sheet, and so on to the smallest sizes of 24, 32, &c. After the sheets of a book have been folded, they are collated by the numeral or letter placed at the foot of the first page of each sheet, in order to ascertain that the work is perfect. The next process to which it is submitted is that of pressing. This is accomplished by means of a hydraulic press. The back of the sheets is then sawed by machine, after which the sewing process commences.

The operation of sewing is conducted with great rapidity, since a female can sew two or three thousand sheets a day. Many modifications of the process occur, according to the size of the book and the style of binding. Thus, the number of strings may be from two to five.

A *sewing-press* consists of a flat bed or board, from which rise two end-bars, connected at the

top by a cross-bar. Each successive sheet is laid flat on the bed of the sewing-press, with the back edge in contact with the strings, then opened in the middle, and fastened to the strings by passing a threaded needle backward and forward through the central fold of the sheet; each thread, after passing from the inside to the out, being made to loop or twist round one of the strings before entering the sheet again. As soon as one sheet is fastened to all the strings, another is laid down on it, and fastened in a similar manner.

The sewer, seated somewhat obliquely in front of this machine, with her left arm passing round the left vertical bar (as seen in the annexed cut), proceeds to sew the various sheets to the bands, her left hand being behind the strings, and her right hand before.

The modern invention of caoutchouc or India rubber binding, it should be remarked, supersedes the necessity of sewing. A flexibility is effected by this kind of binding, greater than can be produced by a sewed book; it also is so retentive as to bind every single leaf securely.

When the book is taken from the sewing-press, an inch or two of each string is left hanging to it; these are afterwards either scraped so thin as to be but little conspicuous, or are employed for fastening the book to its case. The back of the book—that is, the assembled

2*

back-edges of all the sheets—is glued, to increase
the bond by which they are held together.
When the book has gone through one or two
other minor processes, that one succeeds which
is, perhaps, as remarkable as anything displayed
in book-binding; viz. rounding the back and
hollowing the front, as represented in the following cut.

The back of the book being thus rounded, a
groove is thereby formed, into which the mill-
board is adjusted; the covers being fastened by
the strings through the boards.   The book, after

being properly adjusted between two boards, is screwed in a press, with one of the ends projecting a little above the level of the bench. The ends of all the leaves are then cut off while in this position, by means of an instrument called a " plough," the cutting edge of which, in its mode of action, is midway between that of a pointed knife and a plane-iron. The edges are all cut to a perfect level; and the book being reversed, the other end is similarly treated.

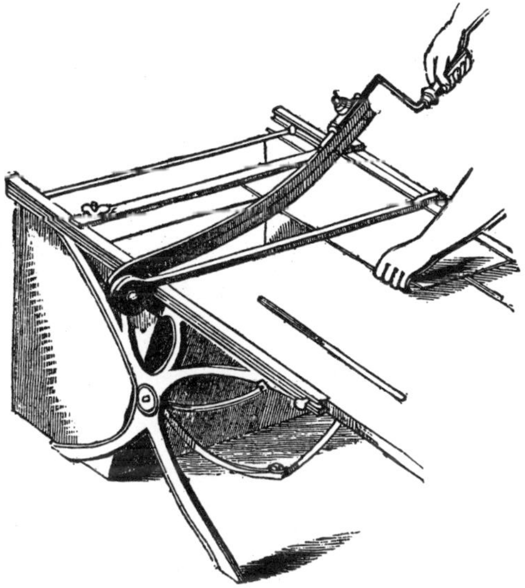

The above engraving represents the machine by which the boards are cut. These shears

are so arranged that they are made to cut
with perfect accuracy, according to any pattern.
The preparatory process for binding in leather
varies somewhat from the foregoing, which
relates to books bound in muslin. The embossing machine, delineated in the following

engraving, is used for stamping covers with
various devices. It is of immense pressure, sometimes amounting to fifty tons. Two of these
beautiful machines, costing $1000 each, con-
structed by Adams of Boston, are constantly in
use in the above establishment. They are both
worked and heated by steam, and are capable of
producing about eighteen impressions each an
hour. The entire amount of machinery used in
this department of the New York Bindery may
be estimated at $15,000. There is also a great
variety of standing presses, from the gigantic

hydraulic to the simple lever power-press. So complete and ample are its appointments, that it is believed no similar establishment can boast superior facilities in this respect in the United States. The number of its employés varies according to circumstances from sixty to a hundred, and sometimes more. So extensive are the facilities of this establishment, that from 800 to 1000 volumes have frequently been bound in a single day.

The various details of the finishing and decorating process it is unnecessary to particularize. The ornaments on the back, sides, or edges of a book, are frequently done by a wheel or " roll," in the manner here represented. The edge or periphery of the wheel has the device in relief, and this, being wheeled along carefully over the surface of the book, leaves a corresponding depression.

The costly bindings in velvet and silk, the gold and silver clasps of expensive bibles, and all the niceties which the connoisseur in book-binding regards with such an admiring eye, we must pass over.

Book-binding has made wonderful advances

during the past ten or fifteen years; the multiplied uses of machinery having, to a great extent, usurped the former slow processes by hand.

We are indebted to the French for the invention of illuminated binding. This is relieved by the insertion of different colored leathers, in imitation of the illuminated MSS. and missals of the middle ages. The effect of this method of inlaying is very rich and beautiful; uniting the attractions of the most elaborate gilding and skill in design with the beauties of the arabesque. By the aid of machinery, this gorgeous style of binding, which formerly was only to be produced at prodigious expense, is now made available at comparatively very moderate cost. Another specimen of ornate binding is that lately introduced in imitation of the antique oak-carving, and iron. The covers are of gutta percha, and present so close a resemblance to the former, that it is difficult to detect the difference between them. Great varieties of devices have challenged the ingenuity and skill of modern book-binding.

The process of gilding the edges of a book is a curious and delicate operation. After the edges are well scraped and burnished with the agate, they are then colored over with red bole or chalk, ground in soap, rubbed immediately dry with fine clean paper shavings, and again well burnished. This gives a richer effect to the gilding, and tends to hide any defects. The gold leaf is then cut into slips, and laid on. When it is required to give an additional degree of beauty and finish to any ancient production, the edges are done in the antique style, by stamping them with flowers or other devices, characteristic of the date of the book. This mode, said to be peculiar to works of the 16th century, is now seldom used. The mode of gilding upon marbled edges, which Dr. Dibdin, in his " Decameron," styles " the *ne plus ultra* of the bibliopegistic art," is another process, demanding great expertness and skill. The effect is very beautiful, for, when finished, the marbling is perceived through the gold, and presents a very striking effect. Landscapes, and paintings of flowers in water colors, are sometimes produced in a similar manner, the luxurious effect of which is dazzlingly beautiful. The picture will not be apparent when the volume is closed, from the gold covering it, but when the leaves are spread out obliquely, it will be at once seen.

It remains only for us to speak briefly of the gilt embellishments, called embossed or arabesque bindings. These are executed with designs cut in plates of brass; after the impressions of which have been made, the gold is rubbed off to display the beauty of the device. Another rich style of ornamental binding is that of silk, satin, or velvet, with decorations in gold and silver. The illuminated style of binding is one of the utmost magnificence, uniting the beauties of the arabesque and gilt ornament with the illuminations of the early missals and MSS. of the middle ages. This mode of binding was formerly produced at prodigious cost; but, although it is now comparatively seldom adopted, it is effected by a much less expensive process—that of inlaying various colored leathers.

By the important aid of modern machinery, a vast improvement both as to accuracy and beauty of workmanship, as well as economy, has been effected. In the New York Book-bindery, the most complete and systematic arrangements exist, so that all these advantages are thus rendered available to their utmost extent. It offers, therefore, peculiar advantages for gentlemen forming or enriching their literary collections, with whom economy is an object—the scale of charges for the various styles of binding being much below the average, while the workmanship is guaranteed of the best possible description. This establishment, which has been in successful operation for about fifteen years, is chiefly devoted to the more elegant and costly styles of book-binding, in its several varieties of velvet, turkey, morocco, russia, calf, and sheep binding, &c.

Fashion, which arbitrates taste in everything else, rules in the matter of book-binding ; successive epochs have had their various peculiarities, and have left on the covers of books the impress of their prevailing styles. During the middle ages, and at later periods, we find books were inclosed in massive covers of oak, grotesquely and sometimes beautifully adorned with carved devices, huge bosses, clasps, &c. There were also others of vellum, hog skin, and sheep skin, with heavy back bands and thick boards, bevelled off towards the edges. Of the more costly styles of the missals we have already spoken. Book-binding scarcely attained to the dignity of an art till within the past thirty years. During this interval, it has made advances commensurate with the progress of the arts of engraving and printing. This increased devotion to the cultivation of literature and the fine arts, is attributable to the fostering care and patronage of men of opulence and taste.

That the book-binding art is susceptible of yet

further improvement will be readily admitted. This is abundantly evident from the beautiful specimens of the art exhibited on some of the works recently issued by the London publishers, and by Mr. Putnam of this city, whose superior taste in this particular, as well as in the typographical excellence of his publications, has obtained such deserved celebrity throughout the United States. Books, as well as their authors, are deserving of good clothing; they are, indeed, not infrequently judged of by the popular eye, more by their exterior embellishment than by the claims of their intrinsic excellence. A genuine book would certainly sell none the less for being well bound; and it is well known that many an inferior literary production has attained even an extended sale, solely in consequence of its having an elegantly embellished cover.

It is a singular fact, that with the advantages of the highest cultivation of art before us, we should revert back to the gorgeous designs of the Gothic ages for the embellishment of our books. How far this preference for the antique is likely to become permanently popular it is difficult to decide. It is, we think, not improbable that it will in a short time give place to a standard of taste more in unison with the modern arts of design. It cannot, however, be denied that great credit is due to the laborious research and artistic skill of Mr. Owen Jones, whose numerous and superb specimens of the illuminations of the mediæval epoch evince such surpassing beauty in their dazzling contrast of coloring, and splendor of the art of printing in gold and silver.

Thus much for the general history of bookbinding. We may now be permitted to refer more particularly to the book-binding establishment of Messrs. Walker.

We have been able merely to give a general outline of the various processes of binding, and must necessarily omit more minute details. The costly bindings in velvet and silk, the gold and silver clasps of expensive illustrated works, including Bibles, Prayers, &c., and all the niceties which the connoisseur in book-binding regards with such an admiring eye, we must pass over in silence. It remains only for us to state, that so complete and extensive are the arrangements effected in this establishment, that the binding of an entire library can be superintended with as much facility as a single volume, while equal accuracy, elegance, economy, and expedition may be confidently relied upon. It is one of the distinguishing peculiarities of the *New York Bindery*, that the several processes of book-binding are all performed within the establishment.

By an admirable distribution of labor in this establishment, large editions of any work, consisting of even 10,000 volumes, can be produced in muslin or sheep binding, in an incredibly short space of time, and in the best possible manner. All the various recent improvements in the art of decorative design and elaborate pictorial and emblematical gilding are here to be found in rich profusion. By the judicious policy of the proprietors, who pay the most liberal terms to their employés, the services of the most skilful artists are secured for the several departments of this establishment. Many of the most superb productions of art that have ever been seen in the United States have issued from this bindery; and as an evidence of its popularity may be mentioned the fact, that upwards of six thousand copies of *Harper's Pic-*

torial Bible and *Shakspeare* have been bound in a variety of splendid emblematic styles, at this establishment. Every variety of plain and ornamental binding is here executed in muslin, sheep, roan, English, French, and American calf, russia, vellum, morocco, velvet, and the inlaid or illuminated styles, as well as those unique and economic styles in half calf and morocco. In all cases the very best description of material and workmanship, combining strength and elegance of finish, will be found to characterize the binding here executed. Librarians connected with colleges and other public institutions, will find it a matter of great economy to apply *direct* to this establishment, as they will thereby effect a saving of twenty per cent., and sometimes more—a deduction of price being made upon large orders so consigned. It will also be to the interest of gentlemen residing at a distance, who sometimes experience a difficulty in getting their binding well done, to pack and direct their orders as above, stating style and price, as they may rely upon their books being well bound, at the lowest prices, and carefully packed and returned with all possible dispatch. In all such cases the owner will be charged with freight, and an order for payment for the binding, on a bank or firm in New York, will be required. The owners of books thus sent should state expressly the route by which they wish them to be returned.

In returning his grateful acknowledgments to his numerous friends and the public for the liberal patronage they have for so many years bestowed upon him, the proprietor takes this opportunity to inform them that he has recently very considerably enlarged and improved his establishment, which he believes to be now as extensive, and to possess as great facilities as any bookbindery in the United States.

His two sons, who have been trained under his special care, aided by talented instructors, are now in partnership with him, and they confidently hope, by their united attention and experience, to give entire satisfaction to their patrons—who may rest assured no expense will be spared in the adoption of every improvement, the employment of the highest grade of workmen, and the most careful selection of stock, while in all instances the most reasonable scale of prices will be adopted.

Music bound on an improved principle, with patent spring backs, in neat and elegant bindings.

For the convenience of persons residing at a distance, the following list of works, with the prices of binding annexed, has been subjoined, in order to facilitate them in forming an estimate of any works of corresponding size and style they may desire to have bound.

VIRTUE'S ELEGANT BIBLE.
    2 vols. impl. 4to., library style, marbled edges. . . $8 00
    Strong calf, marbled edges. 10 00
    Turkey morocco, gilt edges. 16 00
    do. extra do. 20 00

HARPER'S PICTORIAL BIBLE.
    1 vol. royal 4to., library style. 3 00
    Strong calf, marbled edges. 4 00
    Turkey morocco, gilt, gilt edges. 6 50
    do. extra do. 8 00

HARPER'S PICTORIAL SHAKSPEARE.
    3 vols. royal 8vo. calf, gilt, marbled edges. . . 6 00
    Turkey morocco, gilt, gilt edges. . . . 8 00
    do. extra do. 10 00

ALISON'S EUROPE.
    4 vols. 8vo., neat half calf, marbled edges. . . . 2 50
    Full calf, gilt. 6 00

MERRIAM'S WEBSTER'S DICTIONARY.
    Imperial 8vo., strong calf. 2 50
    morocco extra, gilt edges. 4 00

AMERICAN SCENERY.
    2 vols. 4to., half morocco, extra gilt edge. . . . 5 00
    Full Turkey morocco, do. 10 00

GODEY'S AND GRAHAM'S MAGAZINES.

    Half morocco, gilt, marbled edges. $1 00

    Neat calf, gilt,   do. 2 00

    Turkey mor., extra, gilt edges. 3 00

HARPER'S FAMILY LIBRARY.

    18mo., half calf, gilt, marbled edges. 50

    Full calf, gilt. 1 00

AUDUBON'S BIRDS.

    7 vols. royal 8vo., half morocco, gilt edges. . . . 10 50

    Full calf, gilt, marbled edges. 14 00

    Turkey morocco, extra gilt do. 21 00

AUDUBON'S QUADRUPEDS.

    3 vols., royal double folio, half strong binding. . . 15 00

    Half Turkey, morocco, extra. 18 00

    do.   do.   gilt edges. . . . 24 00

    do.   do.   do. joints. . . . 30 00

should be in every library, and form a *vade mecum* or constant companion to every one who aspires to take part in the legislation of this country."—*New Orleans Picayune.*

" This is one of the most important books published in the United States for a long time."—*New York Journal of Commerce.*

" A most complete library in itself, of all that concerns the politics of the country. No individual should be without these volumes. How many hours of idle discussions and senseless debates might be spared to heated partizans, were these books at hand for appeal. We shall have frequent occasion to refer to them."—*Democratic Review.*

" It is, in truth, the best historical narrative of our political statistics that has ever been published on the science of government, of any description whatever, for it furnishes, throughout, the varied and interesting development of the action of a free and enlightened government on the multifarious interests of society, and demonstrates that the latter are more perfectly guarded under the ægis of republican institutions than any other. This work is well written, well printed, and well bound, and must, sooner or later, enter into every library."—*Home Journal.*

" We can say no more, and ought to say no less, of this work, than that it is the most complete constitutional history of the United States that exists, or that can be constructed within the same space. It is indispensable to the library of every American scholar, as a book of reference, and as its title indicates, it is, and always must be, the *Statesman's Manual.*"—*New York Evening Post.*

" The ' Statesman's Manual' is a work of great value, and should be owned and read by every citizen who wishes to know the administrative history of the government under which he lives. It presents information nowhere else to be found in a combined form, of the utmost importance to every American, and absolutely necessary for every public man to possess."—*Boston Post.*

" This publication is invaluable, not only to the politician, but to every citizen : no American library will be complete without it."—*New Orleans Bulletin.*

" No library should be without the book, and if any man has got a house without a library, let him purchase these to begin one. We take it for granted that a work of such unusual interest will be universally called for."—*Graham's Magazine.*

" Few productions of the present day have emanated from the press with stronger claims upon the public patronage than this. It is a noble attempt to present to the great body of the American people, in an available and popular form, the documentary history of the executive government from its commencement under Washington to that of Taylor, together with the details of each administration, in consecutive order, and a mass of important statistical matter not elsewhere to be met with."—*Boston Courier.*

" Here is indeed a work worthy of its title—*national ;* there can be no doubt of its taking its place permanently among works of the highest value."—*Boston Christian Register.*

" To say that these elegant and important tomes deserve a conspicuous place in every private and public library, is not all that should be said—they are indispensable to every lawyer, politician, or intelligent, patriotic citizen."—*Boston Christian Witness.*

II.

NATIONAL AND PERENNIAL GIFT- BOOK.

In one splendidly embellished volume octavo, with rich illuminations in gold and colors, and twelve highly finished portraits of the Presidents, engraved on steel, and bound in a unique and costly style.

THE

TWELVE STARS OF OUR REPUBLIC.

THE NATION'S GIFT-BOOK TO HER YOUNG CITIZENS.

" This elegant volume, which, under the attractive external of an Annual, presents a mass of information relative to our twelve Presidents, must possess interest and value for every American.   The Memoirs of these first men of our nation furnish lessons of practical utility, and fire the youthful mind with a desire to imitate their greatness.   The preliminary sketch, setting forth the causes of our great revolution, is a clear and masterly essay.   The engravings of the Presidents are faithfully executed."—*Lit. American.*

" This is truly a beautiful and valuable book ; handsomely bound, elegantly illustrated, and admirably written.   It contains Portraits and Biographical Sketches of all the Presidents, from Washington to Taylor ; and we hardly know which to commend most, the excellence of the portraits or the justness of the sketches.   Mr. Williams, though a moderate and consistent Whig, is one of the fairest political writers of the day ; and we doubt if the most ardent and ultra Democrat can find a single line in the volume before us to complain of, on the ground of partisan bias.   As for accuracy in dates and statistics, Mr. Williams has no equal in the United States.

" We have not space to dwell upon the merits of ' *The Twelve Stars;*' but the book cannot be praised above its deserts ; and as a ' gift-book' for all classes of readers, it is worth whole cart-loads of fashionable Annuals."—*New York Mirror.*

" This is a splendid gift-book.   It contains sixteen beautiful illustrations, among which are twelve line engravings, representing all the Presidents, from Washington to Taylor ; also four illuminated engravings, as follows: ' The Convention of the Signers of the Declaration,' ' Bunker Hill,' ' The Capitol at Washington, ' The President's House.' In addition to the engravings, there are nearly four hundred pages of letter-press, consisting of much valuable information, especially for young people.   The mechanical execution of the book is beautiful, a remark which may be made on any work coming from Mr. Walker's establishment."—*New York Sun.*

" The publisher, taking advantage of a happy thought, has made an annual of the memoirs of the Presidents, recently issued in other forms, and by adding an illuminated title-page, and views of Independence Hall, the Capitol, and the Presidential mansion, has made a very attractive volume, which is incased in an attractive binding.   A portrait of each President, finely engraved on steel, is given in each volume.   It is, as we have already said, a very valuable book."—*Commercial Adv.*

" An elaborate and accurate collection of highly interesting biographical sketches—in one beautiful volume.   No book can be better adapted for a present to American youth."—*Tribune.*

89

"The frontispiece and other embellishments of the work are superb. It is beautifully printed on fine white paper, and is in all respects equal to our first-class American Annuals. The binding glitters with elegant designs, in harmony with the contents and objects of the volume, and as a gift-book, we have as yet seen nothing that pleases us so well as the Twelve Stars of the Republic."—*Sunday Times.*

"This elegantly bound volume, it will be seen, is a work of great value, and in its present beautiful dress, will form a very appropriate present for a citizen, young or old."—*Observer.*

"This, of all other works issued, is peculiarly adapted for a gift-book to American ladies."—*Globe.*

"It is not to afford amusement for a short time, but instruction for all time to the rising generation. It is a beautifully illustrated text-book. It will be read fifty years hence with as much interest as now. It is got up in the most superb style, inside and out. Art has wonderfully improved in the way of ornamental binding, and this bound book is a good, fair, and full specimen. The designs upon the cover are most chastely and beautifully classical—most ornate."—*Sunday Morning News.*

III.

LIVES OF THE PRESIDENTS.

In one large volume octavo, beautifully printed, and illustrated by twelve portraits, engraved on steel, and bound in muslin, extra gilt, and sheep binding.

THE PRESIDENTS OF THE UNITED STATES,

THEIR MEMOIRS AND ADMINISTRATIONS.

Including an account of the Inauguration of each President, and a history of the political events of his administration, and the transactions of Congress at each session: to which is added, the Declaration of Independence; Articles of Confederation; Constitution of the United States, with notes and decisions; a brief history of the events and circumstances which led to the union of the States, and formation of the Constitution; a synopsis of the Constitutions of the several States; tables of members of the Cabinets, ministers to foreign countries, and a list of members of Congress from 1789 to 1849; statistical tables of revenue, commerce, and population; chronological table of historical events in the United States, etc. By EDWIN WILLIAMS.

"It should be the study of each young man to make himself familiar with his country's history, and the present volume is eminently calculated to promote that object."—*Georgetown Advocate.*

"This highly attractive and useful volume forms not only an elegant picture gallery of our Presidents, it also may be regarded an admirable cabinet history of the political progress of our country. It is a text-book for all who would become familiar with the great leading measures which have emanated from the executive government from time to time, including its foreign and domestic policy."—*Sun.*

"This is an exceedingly valuable addition to political history as it concerns this republic, and should be in every public library, or within the reach of every American. It comprises the annals of each Administration from Washington to Taylor, with a succinct account of the prominent events which have marked the condition of parties throughout the country in the intervals."—*New Orleans Picayune.*

" Mr. Williams has rendered an important service to the country by the publication of this admirable volume, a copy of which should be placed in every public and private library throughout the Union."—*Home Journal.*

" It is a most useful compendium of historical facts in a convenient form for reference."—*Literary World.*

" This work contains a biographical sketch of each of the Presidents, with their respective administrations, and a variety of valuable historical and statistical documents ; and will be found highly interesting to the general reader no less than the politician."—*Tribune.*

" A large, handsome octavo volume. We have here a condensed sketch of the life and administration of each of the twelve Presidents who have been placed at the head of this Republic, since its admission into the community of nations. A variety of important historical and statistical documents are appended, and are here in their proper place. The dozen portraits on steel are really gems in their way. They deserve that the engraver, V. Balch, should have his full meed of merit." —*Albion.*

" The biographies and histories are written with ability and candor, the statistical and documentary portions are compiled with judgment, and the likenesses are well done and truthful. The amount and kind of matter here embodied, cannot fail to make the book highly acceptable to the public, both as a history and a book of reference."—*Jour. of Com.*

IV.

THE ANNALS OF THE AMERICAN REVOLUTION.

In one elegantly printed volume octavo, embellished by seventy-eight illustrations, and bound in muslin, extra gilt, and sheep binding.

SEVENTEEN HUNDRED AND SEVENTY-SIX;

OR THE

WAR OF INDEPENDENCE.

A history of the Anglo-Americans, from the period of the union of the Colonies against the French to the inauguration of Washington, the first President of the United States. By B. J. LOSSING.

" This book appeals to our whole nation. It is a well written and beautifully illustrated history. The style is felicitous, the spirit eminently patriotic. The volume is a faithful chronicle of our Revolutionary period, and will gain for its author high reputation as a historian."— *Literary American.*

" The book is elegantly printed and bound, and the engravings (seventy-eight in number) form in themselves a rare historical gallery of great interest and variety, displaying the originality and taste of the author-artist in this department. As a whole, we have no hesitation in commending this volume as the best popular history of our revolution yet published."—*New York Express.*

" This is a very elegant book, beautifully illustrated with a great number of engravings, and the typography and binding are absolutely faultless. It contains a great amount and variety of information relating to the Revolutionary period of American history, and is a work which will, doubtless, command a very extensive sale."—*Evening Mirror.*

" With regard to the tone and spirit of the volume, the felicity of the style of narrative and reflections, and the great care taken to insure accuracy, as is shown by the author's frequent reference to the best authorities, I am confident that he is entitled to the reputation of a competent and faithful historian."—*Edwin Williams.*

" This is a great national work, the beauties and excellences of which should be studied by every one who would understand the history of human freedom and the inalienable rights of man."—*Albany Spectator.*

" We have heretofore noticed this admirable book in terms of the highest praise. It is a work that should be in every family."—*Godey's Lady's Book.*

---

v.

M. DE TOCQUEVILLE'S GREAT WORK.

In one large volume octavo, handsomely printed on fine paper, and bound in muslin, gilt, or in sheep binding.

THE REPUBLIC OF THE UNITED STATES OF AMERICA.

And its Political Institutions revised and examined. By ALEXIS DE TOCQUEVILLE : Member of the College of France, &c. Translated by HENRY REEVE, Esq. With an original preface and notes, by Hon. J. C. SPENCER. Also an abridgment of the above work, for the use of Schools. 12mo., sheep binding.

" M. De Tocqueville shows himself to be an original thinker, an acute observer, and an eloquent writer. We regard his work, ' Democracy in America,' as by far the most philosophical, ingenious, and instructive which has been produced in Europe on the subject of America. There is no eulogy in it, no detraction, but throughout a manly love of truth. The observations of the author uniformly discover a high degree of acuteness and discrimination. This valuable work cannot be read either in Europe or America without working new and profitable trains of thought."—*North American Review.*

" M. De Tocqueville's able volumes have conferred upon him the highest rank as a political writer ; his practical observations have been tested by the most competent judges,—the Americans and the English ; and his speculative inquiries have been applauded and cited by the first statesmen of the age, whilst they have taken their place amongst the most valuable results of modern political science. But the language of panegyric is not required to draw attention to this book, or to enhance its value ; we only trust that it may be as generally and profitably studied as it has been wisely and conscientiously written."—*British and For. Quarterly Review.*

VI.

TEXT-BOOK ON ROMANISM.

In one handsome octavo volume, embellished with fifty-two engravings, and bound in muslin, extra gilt, or in sheep binding.

THE HISTORY OF ROMANISM,

From the earliest corruptions of Christianity to the present time. With a full chronological table, analytical and alphabetical indexes, and a glossary. A new edition. With a supplement, comprising historical sketches of the late Pope Gregory XVI. and of Pius IX. By JOHN DOWLING, D.D.

The best evidence of the intrinsic value of this remarkably popular work is to be seen in the fact that within the comparatively recent period of its first publication, the extraordinary number of 17,000 copies have been disposed of.

The following is an extract from a letter from the Rev. Dr. Giustiniani, the converted Roman Catholic priest, who is abundantly qualified by education, observation, and extensive study, to testify to the fidelity and value of a " History of Romanism."

" If the reader wishes to be acquainted with the errors of Romanism, he has only to open the pages of Dowling's History. If the reader is anxious to read an epitome of the history of the Popes ; their ambition ; their intrigues ; their avariciousness ; their tyranny ; their superstitions, and their mummeries, he can here find all *proved* and *authenticated* by the most accredited authors of the Church of Rome."

L. GIUSTINIANI.

" It reflects much credit on the skill, patience, industry, and judgment of the author ; he appears very justly to have conceived the idea of a work which has long been regarded as a desideratum by a large portion of those interested in the great controversy with the Romanists."— *Protestant Churchman.*

" We think it an able work, comprising the results of extensive reading and research, and well adapted to fill an important chasm in our literature."—*Lutheran Observer.*

" We regard it as a most important addition to the historical and religious literature of the age. Its contents form a rich storehouse of historical instruction, which should be placed within the reach of every family."—*N. Y. Christian Intelligencer.*

The detached portions of Romish history which were everywhere to be met with, needed to be brought together and presented in systematic order. The reading of *one* book thus becomes better and cheaper than the reading of many."—*Boston Recorder.*

" It it written with the ready, popular eloquence, for which the well known author is distinguished, and cannot fail to arrest attention to the controversy of which it treats. It is a strongly Protestant work, and exhibits the deformities of Popery with great power."—*N. Y. Recorder.*

" The author appears to have brought to the execution of this great work, unwearied industry, genuine and thorough scholarship, and scrupulous fidelity.

RUFUS BABCOCK,
Late President of the Waterville College."

" I have carefully read ' Dowling's History of Romanism,' and can cheerfully recommend it to my fellow Protestants, as an instructive and faithful exhibition of Popery, from its origin down to the present time. It is a book that should be in the hands of every one desirous of obtaining a perfect knowledge of the great Apostasy.

REV. J. WILSON."

VII.

MRS. ELLIS'S POPULAR WORKS FOR THE DOMESTIC CIRCLE.
In one volume octavo, with illustrations on steel, bound in muslin, gilt.

THE FAMILY MONITOR,

Comprising the " Women, Mothers, Daughters, and Wives of England."
By MRS. ELLIS.

VIII.

In one volume, with illustrations on steel, bound in muslin, gilt.
GUIDE TO SOCIAL HAPPINESS,
By MRS. ELLIS.
Containing the " Poetry of Life," "Pictures of Private Life," &c.

IX.

A neat little volume of 216 pages, muslin, gilt.
THE BROTHER AND SISTER,
WITH OTHER TALES FOR YOUTH.
By MRS. ELLIS.

Mrs. Ellis is so well known as an authoress who successfully combines pure lessons of morality and manners with the amusement and interest of fictional narrative, that few other writings are better adapted for that popular form of publication which is insured by cheap, yet well printed and prettily illustrated parts."—*Colburn's New Monthly Magazine.*

" There is some charming writing in these books ; much good sense ; and a few admirable female portraits, that will at once command the interest of the reader."—*Atlas.*

" The style is unassuming, graceful, and fluent."—*Dispatch.*

" The useful and moral purport of this talented lady's writings is extensively known and appreciated."—*Morning Advertiser.*

" There is a solidity about Mrs. Ellis's writings which compels more than attention."—*Lady's Newspaper.*

" We have perused this honest and searching work with much satisfaction, and can confidently recommend it to every mother, who wishes her daughters to become really useful members of society ; and to every young female who has the wisdom to prefer esteem to admiration."—*Christian Advertiser.*

" We do not hesitate to pronounce this one of the best as well as one of the most useful of popular works. Whatever Mrs. Ellis attempts is accomplished in a clear, vigorous, and masterly manner—grappling her subject with a strength and grasp of mind truly astonishing to all, more especially to those who argue that depth of thought and wisdom are the attributes of the sterner sex only."—*Washingtonian.*

" This, we believe, was Mrs. Ellis's first work, and in some respects it is her best. It is a simple, truthful delineation of the joys and sorrows, temptations, duties, and blessings of private domestic life, for the purpose of imparting useful instruction and sound advice. The fiction is wrought with great interest and power, but is always subordinate to a high moral design, and is only assumed as a pleasing medium for the utterance of truths which would lose much of their impressiveness if proclaimed in a didactic form. There are few writers to whom a more cordial commendation can be given by those who regard the interests of morality and religion, as well as the attraction of style and beauty of sentiment, than Mrs. Ellis."—*Evangelist.*

X.

INSTRUCTIVE READING FOR YOUTH.

In one large octavo volume, with nearly three hundred engravings, and bound in muslin, gilt, or in sheep binding.

THE GUIDE TO KNOWLEDGE;

OR, REPERTORY OF FACTS;

Forming a complete library of entertaining information in the several departments of science, literature, and art.

The literary contents of this excellent volume consist of choice selections from the renowned publications of the London " Society for the Diffusion of Useful Knowledge," and comprehend valuable and attractive articles by eminent writers in the several departments of literature, including history, biography, natural history, moral and physical science, fine arts, manufactures, essays, poetry, &c. This popular work presents a more varied, comprehensive, and valuable digest of general knowledge than is to be met with in any single book yet issued from the press. As a proof of its undoubted value, it may be stated that upwards of 20,000 copies have already been sold, while the sales are constantly increasing. It is a work especially adapted for the domestic circle, combining a pleasing variety of subjects, both amusing and instructive, and peculiarly suited for the perusal of youth.

XI.

THE WONDERS OF NATURE AND ART.

A handsome octavo volume, with about two hundred and fifty engravings, and bound in muslin, gilt.

THE WONDERS OF THE WORLD,

IN NATURE, ART, AND MIND;

Comprising a complete library of useful and entertaining knowledge.

The " Wonders of the World" are both more numerous and more various than many may be inclined to suppose ; and it has been the design of the editor to embody all the most remarkable facts in natural history, physical geography, curious customs, eccentric biography, &c. If the great variety in the subjects treated of in any work be considered its recommendation, the present production will not fail of proving universally acceptable ; for it is an attempt to combine in an attractive and portable form, a most extended range of topics of information and amusement. The subjects referred to in the volume comprise among many others, the following :—Atmospheric phenomena, remarkable facts in astronomical science, the most remarkable earthquakes in various parts of the world, caverns, caves, and grottoes, volcanoes, cararacts, eccentricities and anomalies in men and animals, curiosities of the vegetable kingdom, celebrated localities, cities, ruins, &c., ancient and modern, curious customs, manners, and costumes, the Druids, &c.

XII.

In one octavo volume, with thirty engravings, bound in muslin, gilt.

CHRISTIAN MARTYROLOGY,

ILLUSTRATED.

Being an authentic account of the principal persecutions against the Christian Church in different parts of the world, &c.   Compiled from the best sources.

XIII.

In one volume, 18mo., muslin.

THE FATE OF INFIDELITY;

Or the Dealings of Divine Providence with Infidels, &c.   By a converted Infidel.

This book contains sketches of the lives of deists, and exhibits the dealings of Divine Providence with infidels and opposers of Christianity in early and modern times.   It is a book suited for Sabbath Schools and private perusal.   A liberal discount will be made to Christian Ministers, Teachers, and others, who may be disposed to aid in the dissemination of this valuable little volume.

XIV.

POPULAR WORKS ON ODD-FELLOWSHIP.

In three volumes duodecimo, with engravings on wood, and bound in muslin, gilt.

THE ODD-FELLOW'S LIBRARY;

Comprising "Faith, Hope, and Charity," "Friendship, Love, and Truth," and the "Juvenile Odd-Fellow."   Chiefly contributed by Members of the Order.

"This beautiful series comprises a mass of entertaining and instructive reading, elucidatory of the principles of Odd-Fellowship.   It is especially adapted to the families of Odd-Fellows."

"Three uniform volumes, of convenient size, containing articles in prose and verse, illustrative of the principles of Odd-Fellowship, contributed chiefly by members of the Order.   The design of these volumes is extremely praiseworthy, being not only to familiarize the rising generation with those glorious principles now exerting and still to exert so great and good an influence over the world, but also to connect the intelligence and literary progress of the Order, with its progress as an Institution.   Every Odd-Fellow, at least, should possess himself of copies. They are beautifully illustrated by Lossing."—*Ladies' Book.*

xv.

SPLENDID GIFT-BOOK FOR ODD-FELLOWS.

In octavo, beautifully printed on the finest paper, embellished by ten exquisitely engraved illustrations on steel, and a Presentation plate printed in gold and colors, and bound in rich emblematic style. Also, the volumes of the work for 1848, 1849, and 1850, uniform with the above.

THE ODD-FELLOWS' OFFERING,

FOR 1851.

Embellished with elegant engravings, and an illuminated Presentation plate in gold and colors. Contributed chiefly by members of the Order.

" This choice gift-book for 1850, which forms the eighth volume of the series, contains about fifty articles, contributed chiefly by members and friends of the Order, all of the highest moral and intellectual tone. It is beautifully illustrated with eleven elegant engravings, executed in the highest style of the art. The presentation plate is a splendid specimen of illuminated lithographic printing, in thirteen colors."—*Home Journal.*

This valuable annual holds a rank not surpassed, if indeed it is equalled, by any similar work in the United States, in the variety and talent exhibited in the letter-press, the elegance of its embellishments, to say nothing of the exquisite taste of the mechanical execution of the book, in all its parts. This annual is emphatically " of our Order," and we hazard nothing in saying that no brother will find aught that will conflict with our motto of Friendship, Love, and Truth ; but on the other hand, a vast fund from which to draw the means of convincing others of the great value of our institutions. It is a work which is an honor to the literature of the Order, to American literature, to the mechanical arts connected with book-making, and worthy of the most liberal patronage, which we cordially bespeak at the hands of brothers."
—*Gazette of the Union.*

" We have seen but few of the annuals of the season, and this we think the best we have seen. We commend it not only to the large and respectable body for whom it is especially intended, and from whom its contributions chiefly come, but to others. The subjects are neither sentimental nor trivial ; and this remark, strange as it may appear, applies as well to the engravings as the literature of the book."—*American Review.*

" We may safely predict that it will be extensively ' *ordered*' by ' Odd-Fellows' in all parts of the United States. In fact, we should consider him a very odd fellow indeed, who would hesitate to bestow on his wife or sweetheart so beautiful and appropriate a holiday gift."—*Mirror.*

" The articles in this volume are from the first writers of the country, and the dress in which they appear cannot fail to give general satisfaction, and make this annual the great gift of the season. The engravings are well executed, and taken from the designs of the first artists."—*Metropolis.*

" Though its contents are of most interest to Odd-Fellows, they are still eminently readable and attractive for all classes of the community.

Many of them are from the pens of some of the most distinguished writers. The volume is very elegantly published, and contains a large number of excellent engravings."—*N. Y. Courier and Inquirer.*

" This annual forms an excellent volume this year. It has an illuminated presentation plate, and ten very good engravings, the subjects of which, however, are not new. Each of them is illustrated by an original paper. The reading matter of this annual is generally good, but is this year even better than usual. Among the contributors of known reputation are Mrs. E. O. Smith, Mrs. Osgood, Rev. A. B. Chapin, Mrs. Sigourney, Mrs. Kirkland, and others. The benevolent, moral tone which should distinguish a volume designed to circulate among the Order, is well preserved in all the articles. The ' Offering' is well printed, on good paper, and is a volume worthy of its object."—*Commercial Advertiser.*

" It is one of the most elegant annuals of the season ; its contents are varied and deeply interesting."—*Globe.*

" This is truly a magnificent annual."—*Olive Branch.*

" The Odd-Fellows' Offering for 1850 is a very beautiful annual, containing several very handsome engravings, with abundant reading matter of the very choicest kind. This work is justly deserving encouragement, and should be in the hands of every one desirous of having a book both beautiful and useful."—*Philad. Messenger.*

" We most cordially recommend it, not only to brethren of the Order, but to the public generally."—*Philad Sun.*

" This is one of the handsomest, best got up, printed, and bound annuals for the coming season of festivities, and will be taken extensively by the members of the order, and by others. It numbers about a dozen engravings, some of which are eminently beautiful, and two or three of which only seem to have been rather hurried. The contents, all original, show what choice spirits there are in this most benevolent Order. There is in it the very embodiment of talent, charity, and goodness. The book cannot fail of having a large circulation."—*N. Y. Atlas.*

" A most beautiful gift-book, one of the handsomest issued from the American press. It contains literary articles, all original, and chiefly from the pens of members of the brotherhood, for whom it is specially designed. The external appearance is really faultless, being a superb specimen of binding, executed by the publisher. Although this work is dedicated to Odd-Fellows, its contents are of a character which renders it a most acceptable gift-book for all classes."—*Young People's Mirror.*

" Taken as a whole, the work is creditable alike to editors and contributors, publishers, and artists, and we may safely recommend it as an appropriate presentation book, as well for the public at large as for members of the Order."—*N. Y. Com. Adv.*

XVI.

THE BEST BOOK FOR FARMERS.

THE

FARMER'S AGRICULTURAL TREASURY,

AND

GUIDE TO KNOWLEDGE;

Expressly intended to instruct the American farmer how to raise the best crops and the healthiest cattle with the least labor. By the author of the " Book of the Farm," assisted by Professor NORTON, of Yale College, New Haven.

It will embrace every subject of importance connected with Agriculture in all its various branches, both Theoretical and Practical. *Science,* in as far as it has, up to the present time, been made available to *Practice* by *Experiment,* will be treated in its relation to every operation as it occurs in the course of the seasons. The work will be arranged under four distinct heads, representing the seasons, beginning with Winter and ending with Autumn. The following are among the subjects to be treated under the first head, including the Introductory, viz.

INITIATION.

On the best of the existing Methods for acquiring a thorough knowledge of Practical Husbandry ; the Difficulties to be encountered in learning practical husbandry, and on the Means of overcoming them : the different kinds of farming : the persons required to conduct and execute the labor of the farm : the branches of science most applicable to Agriculture : the Institutions of Education best suited to Agricultural students : the evils attending the neglect of Landowners and others to learn practical Agriculture : on observing the details and recording the facts of farming by the Agricultural Student.

PRACTICE—WINTER.

On the treatment of Farm-horses in Winter : the treatment of the Farmer's saddle and harness horse in Winter : the fattening of swine : the treatment of fowls : the rationale of the feeding of animals : on the accommodation of the grain crops in the steading : threshing and winnowing of grain : on the forming of dunghills and composts in winter : on the construction of liquid-manure tanks and carts : sea-weed as manure : on gaulting or claying the soil.

The Work will also embrace many important operations not included in the ordinary routine of farming, such as " *Judging of Land*," " *Stocking of a Farm*," " *Improvement of the Soil*," &c., &c.

The contributions by Prof. Norton will add greatly to the value of the Book, by adapting it to the Soil, Climate, Growth, &c., of our own country. And the united labors of two such distinguished men will make this work one of the most complete and valuable to the American Farmer ever issued from the Press.

The work will be comprised in about 22 Nos. of 64 pages each. It will contain some 18 or 20 engravings on steel, and more than 600 wood engravings, in the highest style of the art.   It will be handsomely printed on fine paper, and sold at 25 cts. a number, or $5 in advance for the twenty-two numbers.   The numbers can be sent by mail at periodical postage.

The subscribers having made arrangements with the publishers of the above work, Messrs. Leonard Scott & Co., to furnish the same to their agents and the public generally, will be happy to receive orders.   The first number will be speedily issued, and the publication will be continued at intervals as rapidly as may be consistent with the proper execution of the work.

E. WALKER & SONS,
114 Fulton Street, New York.

NOTICES.

Professor Norton says, in reference to that portion of the work already written by Mr. Stephens, that " the clear and copious details, the fulness and accuracy of information, the completeness of every illustration, have, in an Agricultural work for practice, never been equalled.   *   *   *   * No farmer, who thirsts for knowledge himself, or who aspires to have his son rise to the true ' post of honor,'—the dignified station of an intellectual and accomplished agriculturist, can justifiably deny himself such a work."

Blackwood's Edinburgh Magazine says, " Those who, like ourselves, take an interest in the diffusion of improved agriculture—scientific and practical—and especially of our own agricultural literature in other countries—will be pleased to learn that the editing of an American reprint has been undertaken by Professor Norton, of Yale College, so well known and esteemed in Scotland, where he obtained the Highland Society's £50 prize for a chemical examination of our native oat, which was published in their Transactions.   He is a worthy representative of the ' country of steady habits' to which he belongs ; and we hope his countrymen will be discriminating enough to appreciate his own character and scientific labors, as well as the value of the book he undertakes to bring before them."

The two poems reproduced here comprised a four-page advertisement that James E. Walker inserted in books and magazines he
bound. The editor is indebted to Carolyn L. Harris of Columbia
University for bringing it to his attention.

LABOR IPSE VOLUPTAS.

JAMES E. WALKER still attends
Personally on his friends ;
Assiduously studies, too,
When binding volumes (old or new),
To give the utmost satisfaction
By merely profiting a fraction
Of what he might, in justice, make ;
Because he'd rather *give* than *take*
Advantage—for his credit's sake.
No person in "THE TRADE" has ever
Surpassed him in his best endeavor
To lessen cost, in every way,
And finish jobs without delay.
EDITION-WORK, 'tis very certain,
He's known to be the most expert in ;
For, when he gets a chance to try
The folding of a single sheet,
Within the twinkling of an eye
His estimate is made complete.
The vast concern he holds is such,
He never finds the work too much
For those he constantly employs—
Both men and women, girls and boys.
The standard works, and all the serials,
He binds with very best materials ;

And executes, with lightning speed,
Whatever 'tis his friends may need.
And how astounding is the fact
That JAMES E. WALKER will essay
With workmanship the most exact
To bind a volume IN A DAY !
In sets of books, his constant care is
To note that pattern never varies.
The richest " tooling " he may see,
He'll match correctly, " to a T ; "
And copy, too, with great precision,
All "letterings," with their division ;
Sew "head-bands" on with little trouble,
In single silken twist, or double ;
And burnish gilded edges bright
As polished steel, exposed to light.
All SUPER-EXTRA WORK required
He makes designs for when desired—
Original in every part,
And veritable Works of Art.
His taste can be denied by none,
For *he inherits it*, as son
Of that respected sire, whose name
First gave this BINDERY its fame.

———

JAMES E. WALKER MAY BE FOUND
AT 20 JACOB ~~AT 14 DEY~~, THE WHOLE YEAR ROUND :
For business duties make him stay
At BINDERY from day to day.
He's seldom half an hour away.

———◆———

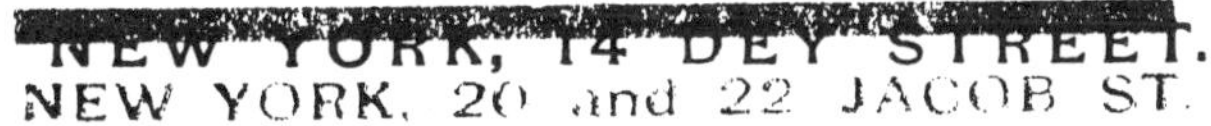

NEW YORK, 20 and 22 JACOB ST.

JAMES E. WALKER has a van, on springs,

Driven by a careful man, who brings

Goods in, for binding or repair—

Takes parcels out, with greatest care,

And *free of cartage* anywhere.

A great advantage, this, to all

Who order ☞ " Man (with Van) to call."

Index

The index includes references to proper names, historic periods, bookbinding techniques and materials, decorative themes, and the services of The New York Book-Bindery. Because contemporary illustrations and decorations are primary sources of information and documentation, they and sometimes their contents have also been indexed. The entire text has been repaged consecutively; index numbers refer to the repagination.